THE BIG JUMP
The Tao of
Travis Pastrana

TRAVIS PASTRANA WITH ALYSSA ROENIGK

ISBN: 978-1-933060-32-3

ESPN books are available for special promotions and premiums. For details contact Michael Rentas, Assistant Director, Inventory Operations, Hyperion, 77 West 66th Street, 11th floor, New York, New York 10023, or call 212-456-0133.

FIRST EDITION

10 9 8 7 6 5 4 3 2 1

To my mom, dad, and the entire family, for your continued love and support—despite all the near heart attacks I've caused. Without you, I never would have made it.

CONTENTS

Travis Pastrana is the only person who scares me. His mind terrifies me at times. But it also excites me.

The last time he was in Oklahoma, we met near my house to ride go-karts and have some fun. Over lunch, he told me about a couple of his latest dreams. Travis thinks of me as his Mad Scientist. If I believe one of his ideas is mathematically impossible, he'll move on to the next idea in his mental file. That day, he told me he wanted to attach one end of a bungee cord to his waist and the other end to a helicopter. Then he would jump his bike over a ramp, wide open in fifth gear. At the peak of his jump, the helicopter would pull him away from the bike.

Next, he told me of his desire to jump out of a plane without a parachute, then catch up with another skydiver who's already jumped. Travis would grab hold and hang on as the other guy deployed his chute. Both ideas are *possible.* And both scare the hell out of me.

Although he's only 23, Travis has redefined our world. He's re-written entire laws of physics. By conquering seemingly impossible challenges like the double backflip, he has opened the door of possibilities wider than we ever dreamed. For him, there is nothing to fear but his own fearlessness. He's focused and dedicated, and he's driven by a passion to challenge the unknown. He influences and inspires. He accepts no limits. Travis pays a high physical tax for the things he does. But his reward is spiritual. He pushes hard and, in turn, lives a fuller life.

I feel rejuvenated when I spend time with Travis. His energy transforms any room he enters. The world is his playground and it's fun to be his playmate. A freak of nature, he uses his incredible athletic ability and vision to challenge his ultimate opponent: the Impossible. I can't wait to see what the Pastrana mutant gene will break down next.

—Mat Hoffman

Crazy | ˈkraze |

ADJECTIVE: Mentally deranged, especially as manifested in a wild or aggressive way; foolish.

Fear | fi(ə)r |

NOUN: An unpleasant emotion caused by the belief that someone or something is dangerous, likely to cause pain or a threat.

Too often, action sports athletes are summed up in one word: crazy. People judge our actions without taking time to learn the thinking behind them. Every trick I learn, every stunt I pull is analyzed. What's the risk? What's the reward? What are the chances I will fall? If I do fall, what are the chances I'll be injured? If I'm injured, will it be worth it? Then I make my decision.

Most people's lives are controlled by fear. But just because something appears scary doesn't mean it is. And vice versa. My friend Scott was afraid of heights. One day he went bridge jumping with some other guys, but when he saw the 40-foot drop, he got scared and couldn't go through with it. So he walked to a lower point, which, it turned out, was above a section of the river that hadn't been dredged for boat traffic. Scott jumped, but his feet sunk into the mud and he drowned in four feet of water. Because of his fear of heights, Scott passed up a jump that seemed terrifying for one that didn't look as dangerous. But he was scared of the wrong thing; his lack of research killed him.

It's interesting how differently people handle fear. I'm constantly shocked that most people aren't aware of why they are scared. I've seen grown men cry while waiting in line for a roller coaster. When I ask them what they're afraid of, they tell me it's the height. Wouldn't it be more logical to be afraid of falling, or of shoddy workmanship? There is no logic to their fear. Athletes in alternative sports break fears down and make them logical.

The term "life-or-death situation" is not a metaphor to me. About a dozen times a year, I put myself in these situations. The clarity and purpose I find in conquering a life-or-death situation is almost euphoric. Time actually slows down. A two-second jump feels like 20, and every sense is magnified. Those of us who have made a career out of these moments find ourselves living 100 percent in that moment. Nothing else matters; in essence, we become free.

Most freestyle riders would rather jump a motorcycle 100 feet over rock-solid dirt than try their first backflip into a soft foam pit. Why? Because the backflip is new, it's unknown. They refuse to accept that a trick they thought was impossible is actually easy and fun. People establish limits early in life and sometimes never learn to think outside that box. The greatest talent to have in action sports is not strength or skill. It's the ability to set your own limits and not be confined by the limits of

THE FIRST TIME I OFFICIALLY
FELT LARGER THAN LIFE.

those who came before you. Great people don't dwell on the failure of others, but learn from their mistakes.

I enjoy the abstract thinking needed to succeed in action sports; I love when a trick doesn't work on the first try, or even the one-hundred-and-first try. I worked on the **Super flip** for a month before I could land it consistently, and now it's one of my favorites. There is nothing more exciting than being the first to figure out a trick. The answer is the easy part. But I figure out the equation.

I do what I want almost every day. I get paid to have fun, and I have found that the more I am willing to fail, the more I succeed. To those who think I'm crazy for taking the risks I do, I ask you this: What would you sacrifice so you could wake up every morning with a smile on your face and sincere excitement for what the day will bring?

There's only one way to find out: Just grab the handlebars and jump.

—Travis Pastrana, May 2007

Super Flip (Soup•er•flip)
NOUN: A trick combining a Superman (in which the rider grips the handlebars with his body and legs flying out behind him) and a backflip. Pastrana invented the super flip in 2005.

LEARNING TO JUMP

If you say you're going to do something, do it.

When I was two, my folks bought me a go-kart. My older cousins were scared to ride it, but I hopped right in. No shoes, no helmet, no fear. I flipped it the first day. My parents must have anticipated that, because it was the only go-kart in the neighborhood with a roll cage. It was sweet. It had a 10-horsepower motor and topped out at 40 mph. I loved crashing that thing almost as much as I loved racing it. When I was about two-and-a-half, I drove it through our garage door. I've been crashing stuff ever since.

I got my first motorcycle for Christmas when I was four. When I was injured and couldn't ride it, my best friend, Jim DeChamp, and I would build go-kart jumps. We could turn anything into a competition.

"Hey Jim, I bet you can't jump off that loading dock!"

"Bet I can."

"Bet I can jump farther than you."

"Bet you can't."

I was competitive from the start, but I was a different kind of competitive. I wanted to win, but I also wanted to make up the rules. I started racing motocross when I was four, and I did well right away. When I was six, I raced 12- and 13-year-olds at local events. My parents entered me in the divisions for older kids, which wasn't popular with the other parents. They protested at almost every race I entered. They didn't think it was fair for their sons to lose to a kid half their age. Because of the protests, I didn't receive half the trophies I earned in those years. But I didn't care. I didn't need a room full of trophies to tell me what I'd won. For me, racing was all about having fun. And win or lose, I had as much fun as any kid on the track.

But even when I won, I wasn't always winning popularity contests. Neither were my parents. The games my dad and I played might have had something to do with that.

If I had just shown up at races, competed my heart out, won, and gone home, I would have gotten bored with racing. My parents knew that. So my dad invented games to make races more competitive. Sometimes he'd have me line up at the start gate facing backward. Other times, to practice getting a quick start, he'd have me race the first two turns, then go back to the start line, take off again, and catch up. Once in a while, he even offered the other kids $10 if they could get the hole shot by beating me off the start and into the first turn.

Then there was my dad's favorite game. I would get to a race all excited and confident. He'd see that and say, "Trav, I want you to win by as much as you can." Sure, Dad! I'd tear out of the start and get a huge

VITALS

Travis Alan Pastrana

Born: October 8, 1983

Hometown: Davidsonville, Maryland

Dad: Robert Pastrana

Mom: Debby Pastrana

I MUST HAVE BEEN ON SANTA'S NICE LIST IN 1987 (TOP LEFT). I TORE THAT BIG BOX OPEN AND COULDN'T BELIEVE IT—A NEW MOTORCYCLE. "I CAN'T RIDE THIS!" I TOLD MY PARENTS. THEN I PUT ON MY NEW HELMET AND RODE AWAY. I STARTED RACING A FEW MONTHS LATER.

I WAS NEVER CONTENT TAKING
THE SAFEST LINE AROUND THE
TRACK. I MIGHT HAVE BEEN LITTLE,
BUT I WANTED TO GO BIG.

A TALE FROM THE CARNIE

By Ronnie Renner

I first met Travis in 1995. I was 18 (he was 11) and I was an intermediate local racer in Florida. Travis, of course, was already a Mini Rider Phenom. We were at the famous Croom OHV Park in Brooksville, Florida, and I was doing my typical practice routine. While I was warming up, I saw this little kid ripping across the pit like a madman. I was on my own program but kept peeking over to see what the little punk was up to. I saw him popping in and out of the trees and couldn't resist following him.

When I got there, I saw him jump this insane cliff jump. He saw me watching and rode over to tell me the jump was "easy." With that in mind, I turned around, shifted up a gear, and hucked it up this 90-degree cliff. I made it to the top, but hadn't thought past that point, so when I landed, I quickly found myself navigating my bike through a maze of trees. I snagged a tree with my handlebars and hit the dirt. Not wanting to be completely embarrassed in front of an 11-year-old kid, I picked that bike up super fast so no one would see I had crashed. The worst part? We've been friends for years now, but Travis doesn't even remember riding with me that day. What a little rock star!

DAD SPEAKS

Travis' mom hated those games. She would get so mad when she saw me walk out onto the course. But the other kids loved them. Travis didn't think so, but they did. I gave them a chance to win. They didn't care how they beat Travis. A trophy was a trophy. We had so much fun at those races.

SIZE MATTERS

Motorcycles are classified by engine size, and they are measured in cc's, or cubic centimeters. Races are divided into classes based on engine size.

lead. Then, halfway through the race, he'd run onto the course and stop me. And hold my bike. If I had a 20-second lead, he'd hold me until the second-place kid passed me and was 20 seconds ahead. With my adrenaline pumping, those 40 seconds felt like an eternity. "Okay," he'd say as he released me, "catch back up!" I loved that game, but I rarely caught up. I lost so many races because of that game. But I didn't care about the trophy. I cared about the challenge.

I was a couple of weeks shy of my 12th birthday when I lined up for my first race in the **125cc division**. Even though the rules stated that riders must be 12 to jump from 80s to 125s, I talked the organizers at a race in Kentucky into letting me move up. "I don't want a trophy, I don't want points, I just want to race," I said. About halfway through the race, I was in second place and tried to pass the leader. But the kid sideswiped me and sent me cartwheeling off the track. I got up quickly and got back on the bike. I rode as hard as I could, caught back up with him, and knocked him down. I was so small I could barely reach the foot pegs, but I wanted him to know I belonged there.

At about this same time, my dad and I stopped playing games. Instead, I started throwing freestyle moves off the jumps more frequently. If I was way out in front at a big race, I would throw a whip over the final jump or do a no-footer or one-hander over a hit. For years, riders had been throwing whips during races or taking a hand off over a jump, but as far as I know I was the first to take both my hands and feet off the handlebars. No one had seen a rider let go with both hands and feet at the same time, and I had been doing it in races since I was 10. I also started throwing nac-nacs and can-cans, moves that most riders thought were impossible. All I was trying to do was keep myself from getting bored.

I was constantly looking for opportunities to spice up a race. In 1993, at an amateur national race called Gatorback, I had a huge lead coming into the final lap on the first of two motos. At the side of the course was a big jump. Everyone else was jumping it, but taking an easy line. I thought it looked fun, so I launched it. The problem was I had way too much speed, so I flipped over the handlebars on the landing and knocked myself out cold. Before the second moto, my parents pulled me aside and, for the first time, asked me not to do something.

Gatorback (Ga•tor•back)

NOUN: Gatorback Cycle Park in Gainesville, Florida, is one of the most famous motocross tracks. Since 1971, Gatorback has hosted Winter Nationals (also known as the Winter Olympics), the year's first major amateur race.

PIT STOP

In 1969 and 1970, when my uncle, Alan Pastrana, played quarterback for the Denver Broncos, NFL rules stated that the quarterback was the only person allowed to call a time out. At the end of a late-season game, he was hit by Baltimore Colts defensive end Bubba Smith and knocked unconscious. While he lay on the field, time expired and the Broncos lost. The next year, the rule was changed to allow any player on the field to call time out.

"You can't hit that jump again," they said. All of my sponsors were at the race and my parents were struggling to make ends meet. It didn't look good to the sponsors when I crashed out of races for completely avoidable reasons—especially when I was in the lead. "Okay," I said. "I won't hit the jump." And I didn't. I won by a landslide, but was so bummed that I pouted the whole way home. I was probably the only kid who ever cried because he won a race. My parents couldn't take it. "We're sorry, Travis!" my mom finally said. "Next time, you can do the jump." That was the last time they ever told me I couldn't do something on the track. They realized winning wasn't important if I wasn't happy with the way I won.

The next year, in 1994, at a **Budds Creek** national, there was a triple jump no one was hitting—none of the pros, none of the guys on the 250s. It was a big jump and everyone said it was impossible. So of course I wanted to try it. I had a huge lead in the final, so on the last lap I rode off the track, around a tractor, through the event banners, across a stream and hit the jump—and landed it. The crowd went absolutely crazy. But another rider passed me while I was setting up for the jump and I couldn't catch back up. I lost the race.

Afterward, my dad met me in the pits. "Travis, you're an idiot," he said. "But you had fun. That's what matters." The other parents didn't understand how my folks could allow me to lose a race like that—and risk injury on such a dangerous jump. But my parents just smiled and ignored it. They were there to see that I had a good time. If I worked hard and tried my best, they supported me. If all I had to show for my racing career was a bunch of trophies, I wouldn't feel very successful. But I had more fun than any kid out there. And win or lose, I learned how to compete—and

Budds Creek (Budds•Creek)

NOUN: Budds Creek Motocross Park, located in southern Maryland, calls itself "America's motocross capital." Barely a weekend passes without a major amateur or pro race taking place, and many riders call Budds Creek their favorite place to ride.

PEOPLE THOUGHT IT
WAS IMPOSSIBLE TO
TAKE BOTH YOUR
HANDS AND YOUR FEET
OFF THE BIKE DURING A
RACE. I WAS DOING IT
WHEN I WAS 10. GOOD
THING NO ONE TOLD ME
IT WAS IMPOSSIBLE.

GROWING UP, I WAS
MOST CONFIDENT WHEN
I WAS ON MY BIKE. I FELT
UNSTOPPABLE AT TIMES,
AND THAT CONFIDENCE
FILTERED INTO EVERY
ASPECT OF MY LIFE.

have a hell of a good time doing it. Like most kids, I learned my most valuable lessons when I was very young.

When I was about three, I went to a local swimming pool with my parents. I was watching the older kids jump off the high dive, and I said I wanted to do it. My dad helped me climb to the top, but when I walked out onto the platform and looked down, I realized it was really high. I changed my mind. "I don't want to jump anymore," I said.

"Sorry," he told me. "You said you were going to jump. If you say you're going to jump, you have to jump." No way I was jumping. So I started to cry. It's the only time I remember crying because I was scared to do something. So my dad picked me up and threw me in. Smack! I did the biggest, most painful belly flop. Then I cried some more. "See," he said. "You should have jumped on your own." At the time, I didn't understand the lesson he was teaching me. And he didn't know that his stunt would get us thrown out of the pool by a lifeguard who threatened to call child services.

Later that year, my dad and a bunch of his friends were at this bridge near our house. My friends and I jump it all the time now, but I was only three at the time and still had not recovered from the high-dive incident. All the grown-ups were jumping, and when I saw how much fun everyone was having I yelled, "I wanna jump!" My dad was skeptical. "Are you sure?" he asked. "It's pretty high. And if you say you're going to jump, then you have to jump. Remember?"

"I'll jump! I'll jump!" I said. I don't know if my dad believed me, but he helped me climb the guardrail. As soon as I looked over the side, I changed my mind. I was only three feet tall, and that drop looked enormous! "I'm not jumping," I said. "I'm not—." Before I finished my sentence, my dad threw me off the bridge. I screamed all the way down, landed in the chilly water, then swam to the edge of the river and pouted.

From that day on, if I said I was going to do something, then dammit, I did it. If there is anything I've learned from my dad, it's that you stick to your word. I will do anything to live up to my word or keep a promise. But my mouth has been known to get me into trouble. Sometimes I use it to motivate myself—especially with training. If I say I'm going ride my road bike 100 miles tomorrow, then I have to do it, no matter what. Sometimes I talk way above what I think I can do, just to make sure I try as hard as I can. In freestyle, you say you're going to try something—like a double backflip—and either you get lucky and land it or you crash. But you still did it.

Racing is different. Just because you say, "I'm going to win," doesn't mean you will. Usually when I talk about winning, I end up taking more risks, which reduces my chances of making it to the finish. Sometimes I say things before I realize what I'm saying. Then I'm forced to make good on my word even if I know it's not possible. That's what scares my parents most. They hate to hear me trash-talking or making bets. From their viewpoint, nothing good ever comes of it.

I was nine years old the first time my mouth got me into trouble on a bike. I was taking warm-up laps before the Ponca City motocross race. There was a 100-foot jump on the course and Kevin Windham, then 15 and already one of the best riders in the sport, was the only rider trying to gap it. The jump was at the end of the track and the landing was on the other side of the finish line. Your bike might explode and you might have a few broken bones, but you could hit the jump, crash, and still win.

I was talking with Guy Cooper and watching Windham hit the jump. Guy was the 1990 AMA 125 national champion and one of my favorite riders. He is also the uncle of my good friend Kenny Bartram. I wanted to impress Guy, so I started talking trash. "I can jump that," I said, expecting him to tell me I was crazy. Instead, he said, "All right, kid. Jump it. I'll watch."

ONE HOT HAND

Rarely does my betting habit translate to a betting habit. Except when I'm in Vegas. The blackjack tables call my name. But, I never, ever win. Except one time.

I was in town for a Suzuki dealer show in 2006 and another company hired a *Playboy* model to pose next to their product. She saw me and started screeching, "Oh my god! Oh my god! Travis Pastrana!"

I was like, "Oh my god! Oh my god! She knows my name!"

Later that night, I lost $200 in six hands of blackjack. So I called it a night. I was walking back to my room when I passed her in the casino.

"Hi, Travis! Where are you going?"

"Oh, I just got here," I lied. "I was about to sit down. Want to join me?"

"Sure! But I don't have any money."

"No problem. Here's $200. Just promise to give me half of anything you win."

She was the worst blackjack player I've ever seen. She never looked at the table. She doubled down when the dealer was showing face cards. If she was showing 17? "Hit me!" She pissed off everyone at the table.

And she won $1,200.

Good investment, if you ask me.

THIS PHOTO WAS TAKEN THE DAY I ENTERED MY FIRST RACE. I COULDN'T WAIT TO GET OUT ON THAT TRACK.

Great. I was sure I couldn't make the jump. Windham was hitting it on a 125 and barely clearing it, and I was on an 80. Reality hit. There was no way I could make that jump. I took a practice lap to see what kind of speed I could get coming into the takeoff. The answer: not enough. But I said I would do it, so I had to hit it.

On the final lap of the first of two motos, I came around the last turn and saw Guy standing next to the takeoff. He was watching to see if I would live up to my word. I thought, "This is going to hurt." It was weird to know I wasn't going to make that jump, that I was going to crash and be in a lot of pain, and still step up and do it. That probably makes me sound like a complete idiot. Five seconds before I hit that jump, I was 100 percent sure I had a zero percent chance of success. But I had put myself into that situation and I needed to accept the consequences. So I hit the jump and launched damn near 100 feet.

Fortunately, I got lucky. When I landed, the tires blew, the forks bent under, the handlebars broke, and the bike collapsed under me. It was the softest crash landing I had ever experienced. I flew off the bike, flipped a couple times, and face-planted into the dirt. When I stood up, I didn't have so much as a bruise. I looked toward the sidelines, and there was Guy with a big grin on his face. I had come close. Real close. I smiled and waved at Guy. "I did it!" I said, as my dad dragged the pieces of my bike off the track. I told my dad that if I was behind in the final, I could hit that jump and crash into the lead.

"Please don't do that," he said.

You'd think that crash would have taught me to keep quiet. But I soon opened my mouth again. And once again, I set myself up to try a stunt I knew I couldn't do.

The biggest, gnarliest jump on the Motocross circuit is LaRocco's Leap at Redbud in Buchanan, Michigan. The takeoff sits several feet below ground level, so you're doing a step-up to a 120-foot gap that ends in a set of triples. It's named after local rider Mike LaRocco, and only few riders have attempted to land it on a 125cc bike. Of course, I had to be one of them.

In 2000, I was still racing the 125cc circuit and went to Redbud for a race. Ernesto Fonseca was hitting the jump on a new four-stroke Yamaha 250, and barely reaching the landing. We were racing the same class, but his bike had about eight more horsepower than mine and he weighed 150 pounds to my 185. When I came out for the first practice, the other guys started in on me. "Hey, Pastrana, I thought you were the jumper. I thought you could jump that step-up." I was like, "Dude, I can jump anything Ernesto can jump."

Wait.

That's anything Ernesto could jump *if* we were on the same bike. I knew I couldn't jump LaRocco's Leap on my 125, but of course I had to open my mouth. I lined up for my first practice run knowing I had to give it a try. When I came to a section where the track formed a U, I turned off the track and headed through the grass to the fence, giving me a long straightaway. As soon as the fans saw what I was doing, they were on their feet. It was only practice, but they knew they were about to watch me attempt something no one had done. And now that everyone was watching, I couldn't back out. So I pinned the bike and headed for the takeoff. By the time I hit the track, I knew I didn't have enough speed, but I had passed the point of no return.

Just like the last time, I came much closer to clearing the jump than I thought I would, but I smacked into the backside of the landing. It takes a lot to explode a factory motorcycle rim, but when my front tire hit, the wheel exploded like a bomb and sent me flying over the handlebars. I flipped once, landed on my feet, and then did a belly flop onto the dirt. No broken bones, not a scratch. The crowd went nuts. I looked up from the ground and thought, "Well, at least I did it."

As I walked off the track dragging my wrecked bike toward the pits, I knew half the guys were thinking, "That guy is an idiot," and the other half were thinking, "That guy is crazy." They were probably both right. But what mattered was that I said I was going to do something, and I did it. In racing, you're not always going to win. In freestyle, you're not always going to land a trick. But if you do what you said you'll do, then you never fail. Well, kind of.

THE JUMP TO FREESTYLE

Every opportunity offers a new path in life. Remember, there are no wrong turns.

Most of the opportunities in my life have come when I least expected them. My freestyle career started that way, and I have a group of Crusty guys to thank.

I was 13 and racing on Suzuki's amateur program. Even though I was still three years from turning pro, I was invited to test with Team Suzuki in Florida during the week leading up to the 1996 Daytona Supercross race. The guys from the Crusty Demons of Dirt were also in town filming for what would become their third video, *Crusty 3*. I didn't know them, but I had seen the videos so I definitely knew of them—Seth Enslow, Anthony Pocorobba, Larry Linkogle. They were gnarly. They were tough. They were freestyle before freestyle was a sport.

While we were testing, the Crusty guys built dirt jumps not far from the racetrack. Back then, a group of riders hitting huge jumps and doing tricks was an attention-grabber, so when the Crusty guys showed up, a bunch of us racers pulled up lawn chairs and watched them jump. The racetrack was in a swampy area near Daytona, in the middle of nowhere, and it wound around several lakes. The Crusty guys had built a tough 110-foot jump over one of the lakes. It had a short run-in with a big take-off and a super-short landing. As soon as you touched down, you had to make a sharp turn to keep from crashing into another lake. Basically, if you landed short or long, you and your bike were taking a dip in a lake full of alligators. I know that didn't make the jump any harder, but it sure seemed cool.

After about an hour, not a single rider had hit that jump. They were taking a lot of practice runs and hitting smaller jumps, but no one was jumping over the lake. Someone needed to step up.

"You want to go back to the track, Travis?" my dad asked.

"No. I want to do that jump," I said, pointing toward the lake.

"Do you think you can make it?"

"Yeah, of course."

"Well then, do it."

The guys had no idea who I was and never saw me coming. I grabbed my bike, got a good run at the jump, and launched over the lake. I didn't take a single test run, just hit it cold. I landed perfectly between the two lakes, waved at the Crusty guys, and rode back to my dad. They

Crusty Demons of Dirt (Crus•ty•De•mons•of•dirt)

NOUN: A group of tough, tatted motocross riders who appear in videos of the same name. The group includes distance jumpers (Trigger Gumm), freestyle riders (Nate Adams), and a long list of questionable characters.

THE CRUSTY DEMONS OF DIRT (FROM
LEFT): MAD MIKE JONES, LARRY
LINKOGLE, DANA NICHOLSON, BUBBA,
JON FREEMAN, AND SETH ENSLOW.
FACES ONLY A MOTHER COULD LOVE.
JUST NOT MY MOTHER.

were stunned. A little kid just showed them up. They came running after me, asking my name. "Where did you learn how to jump like that?" they wanted to know. "Maryland," I said.

Of course, now that the kid had landed the jump, the older guys had to give it a try. Seth Enslow went first; he came up short, flipped over the handlebars, and hit his throat on the dirt so hard that he could barely breathe. Anthony Pocorobba jumped next; he overshot the landing, flipped off the bike, and snapped his ankle. Seth and Anthony were the two main Crusty riders, and they were supposed to film for the rest of the week. Now they were in the hospital and out of commission. "Well, kid," one of the other guys said, "you're up. Let's see what you've got." I was psyched. The Crusty crew wanted to watch me jump!

I rode back to the takeoff and hit the jump over and over—one-hander, no-footer, no-handed lander. Over the next hour, I pulled every trick I knew. On one jump, I got so excited that I overdid it and landed in the second lake. I hauled my bike out and called it a day. As I said goodbye to the Crusty guys and headed back to the test track, they told me I should fly out to California to film with them some time.

Right. Like that would ever happen.

Two days later, back home in Maryland, my parents got a phone call.

"No way!" I heard my mom say to my dad. "Have you seen those tattoos? Those guys are scary. And too old. No way my 13-year-old son is going to California alone with them."

What?! The Crusty guys had called. Already! They were planning a film shoot in the California desert and needed two riders. But there was no way my mom was going to agree to this. My parents were used to me traveling by myself, but this was pushing it. To my parents, this was even scarier than my solo trip to Zimbabwe a year earlier.

On that trip, I went with a couple of kids a few years older than me. We met up with adults who organized the race once we got there, but we were pretty much on our own. I broke my wrist a couple days before leaving, but decided to go anyway. The day we arrived, a bunch of us went out on a boat. We saw crocodiles and hippos lying on the shore, but it was so hot we started doing flips into the river. First, we checked the depth finder to see if there were any creatures swimming underneath us. When it looked clear, I jumped—cast and all.

When we got back to shore, I decided I'd had enough of that cast, so my friends helped me cut it off. Then I crashed at the race, jacked up my wrist, and re-broke my thumb. Snapped it right in half. Guess cutting

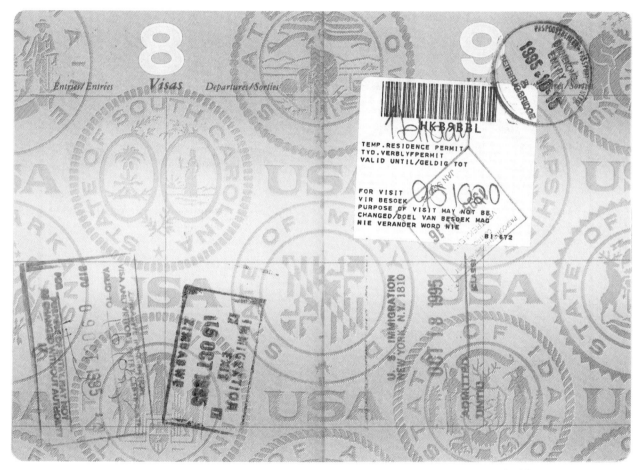

I WAS A WELL-TRAVELED 12-YEAR-OLD. THERE AREN'T TOO MANY KIDS WITH STAMPS FROM ZIMBABWE IN THEIR PASSPORTS.

off the cast wasn't such a bright idea. Traveling like that made me grow up quickly. I was mature from a young age. At school, I was quiet and shy. I was a dork. I still am. But the motorcycle was my sanctuary.

When I rode, it didn't matter what I looked like. I was a rock star. Kids looked up to me and it gave me confidence. Because of that, top motocross riders act like they're 18 when they're still little kids. Unfortunately, when they're 30, they still act like they're 18. I'm only 23, so I should be 18 for a while.

When I was a kid, my parents never had to tell me to go to sleep or

"MOTOCROSS RIDERS GROW UP FAST. WE ACT LIKE WE'RE 18 WHEN WE'RE KIDS. UNFORTUNATELY, WHEN WE'RE 30, WE STILL ACT LIKE WE'RE 18."

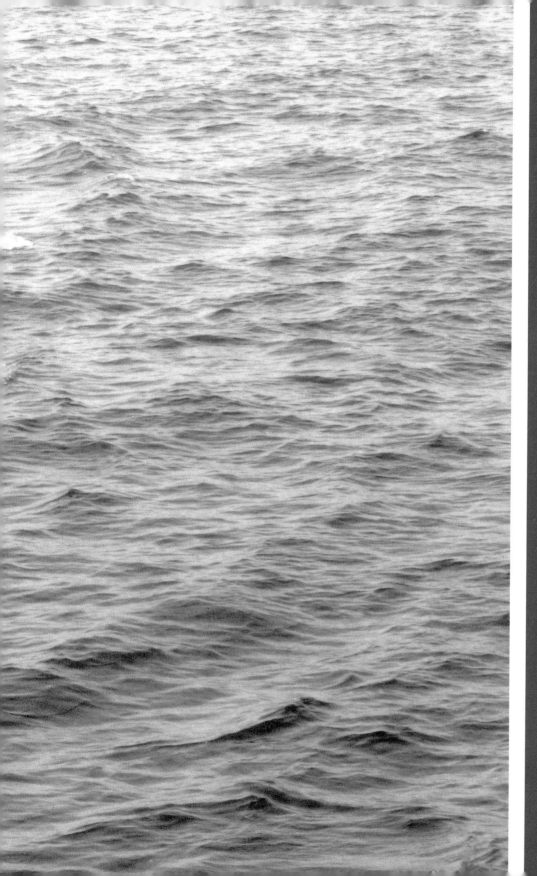

FLOATING DOWN
ZAMBEZI RIVER WITH
A FEW FRIENDS.
ANOTHER AVERAGE
DAY IN THE LIFE OF A
12-YEAR-OLD
MOTOCROSS RIDER.

do my homework. I never had a curfew or a lot of rules because they weren't necessary. I worked hard because I wanted to, not because my parents told me to. In school, I was the teacher's pet. I always turned in my homework early, never talked during class, and was a straight-A student. My dad preached respect and hard work—those were my rules. The consequences of violating my parents' trust was simple and far too high: no more racing.

In sixth grade, my parents pulled me out of school. It was a tough

NAME *Travis*   GRADE *2*

EXPLANATION OF EVALUATIVE CODES

ACH - Achievement Codes indicate the student's academic accomplishment in comparison with grade level expectations.

    A = 90-100; B = 80-89; C = 70-79; D = 60-69; E = 59 and below

EFF - Effort Codes indicate the student's functioning in comparison with his/her individual ability.

    S = Satisfactory; N = Needs Improvement

SUBJECTS	NOV. Ach	NOV. Eff	JAN. Ach	JAN. Eff	APR. Ach	APR. Eff	JUN. Ach	JUN. Eff
Reading	B	S	B	S	B+	S	B+	S
Language	B	S	B	S	B+	S	B+	S
Spelling	A	S	A	S	A-	S	A-	S
Mathematics	A	S	A	S	A	S	A	S
Social Studies	A	S	A	S				
Science			A	S	A	S	A	S
Computer			S	S	S	S	S	S
Music	A	S	A	S	A	S	A	S
Physical Ed.	A	S	A	S	A	S	A	S
Art		S		S		S		S
Handwriting		S		S		S		S
Religious Ed.		S		S		S		S

A ✓ INDICATES IMPROVEMENT NEEDED

STUDY HABITS	NOV.	JAN.	APR.	JUN.
Listens Carefully				
Follows Directions				
Works For Accuracy				
Does Neat Work				
Works Well Independently				
Works Well In A Group				
Completes Class Assignments				
Completes Homework Assignments				

CITIZENSHIP				
Is Courteous and Considerate				
Practices Fair Play				
Practices Self Control				
Assumes Responsibility				
Observes Rules				
Accepts Constructive Criticism				
Respects Rights and Property of Others				

ATTENDANCE

	November	January	April	June
ABSENT	2	3	5	1
TARDY	0	0	0	0
PRESENT	46	42	37	43

decision. My mom is very education-oriented, but she did not want to homeschool me. She wanted me to have the full experience. Still, I was missing so many classes traveling to races that my grades were suffering, so she didn't have any choice. I actually liked homeschool. My mom was a great teacher and it allowed me to work at my own pace, which was faster than a regular school would allow. I never took a summer off and earned my high school diploma at 15. My parents trusted me. But if I wanted to go on the Crusty trip, I had to do something less than trustworthy.

I was scheduled to fly to California the next week and test with FMF, a sponsor who makes exhaust systems for my bikes. My dad nonchalantly dropped that information into conversation with my mom. "Well, he can't

TALK ABOUT A GOOD-LOOKING KID. AND SMART, TOO (OPPOSITE). BUT MY TRAVEL SCHEDULE CAUGHT UP WITH ME AND IN THE SIXTH GRADE, I STARTED HOME SCHOOL. ELEMENTARY SCHOOL IS THE ONLY GRADUATION CEREMONY I ATTENDED.

LMOC

When I'm hurt, I have a lot of free time. Sometimes I write stories or movie scripts or think up new tricks. When I was 15, I also earned a couple years' worth of college credits in my spare time. (My uncle was a football coach at Anne Arundel Community College, so I enrolled there.) I tested straight into sophomore-level classes and got a lot of funny looks from the other students. "Who's the little kid?"

I didn't go to college to earn a degree. I simply wanted to educate myself on subjects that interested me. Most of my friends went to college just to get a diploma. They skipped class and did just enough to get by. What's the point? I liked writing, and even wrote a column for *Racer X* magazine, so I took speech and journalism classes. I hated them. The professors wanted to fit every person into the same box. They told me how to write, how not to write, what rules to follow. I write for expression, not to follow rules. I switched to English classes. Much more my style.

I was a straight-A student in college. I have a 4.0 GPA but I'm two years short of graduating. I've never had time to go back. I'm sure there are a lot of reasons why I could use a diploma, but I can't seem to think of one right now.

WORLD OF WONDER
PRE·SCHOOL
1986
MRS ZIMMERMAN
MRS SCHWAB

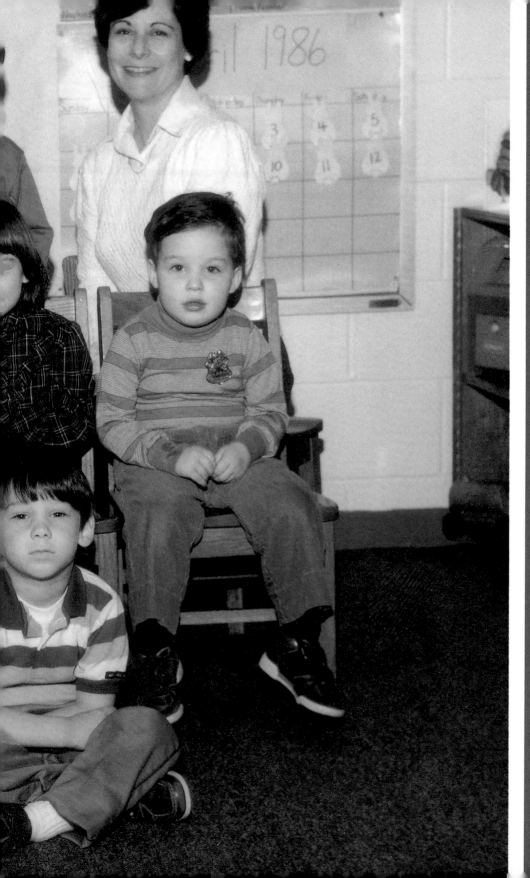

THERE I AM, FRONT AND CENTER. I WONDER IF I'M DAYDREAMING ABOUT BACK-FLIPPING A DIRT BIKE.

UN FILM DE
TRAVIS PASTRANA

Names are not (totally) representative of actual people. But they are representative of my lack of creativity for making up character names.

[Scene: Suzuki test track, a hot, dusty, forsaken place in the middle of the desert. STEVE wipes out in a cloud of dust. When the cloud clears, he lies wrapped up under his bike as blood drips from his arm through a ripped part of his jersey.]

STEVE: [to himself, in a sarcastic tone] Let's race Supercross again. It'll be so much fun.

[TARAH approaches]

TARAH: You don't have time to be lying around. We have to test your new NASCAR this afternoon. We scheduled you for the foam pit tonight and you haven't gone to the gym yet.

STEVE: Gee, that all sounded like so much fun just a few hours ago.

TARAH: Want some cheese with that whine? You are up shit's creek without a paddle. But I've seen you pull through worse.

STEVE: You really think I can pull this off?

TARAH: Honestly, you have stretched yourself thin before, but this definitely takes the cake. You are screwed.

STEVE: There is one positive. [He smiles.] At least I won't be the one who is embarrassing myself by trying to drive an F1 car.

[TARAH gives STEVE the finger. STEVE gets on his bike. Cue action montage to "Eye of the Tiger." Montage starts with STEVE racing Supercross, throwing freestyle tricks, some shots of hard-core training, and ends with a guy shaking his head in disapproval as STEVE flies by in a stock car.]

go anyway," he said. "He has to test." In the same city as the Crusty trip. (He left out that part.) To me, alone, he said, "Son, do what you want. Have fun. Be safe. And you better not get hurt, because if you do, I'll be divorced when you get home." I called the Crusty guys and told them I'd be out within the week. Then I packed my bags, kissed my mom goodbye, and flew to Los Angeles.

When I landed at LAX, I was met by the craziest group of guys I'd ever seen in my life. I can't tell you how out of place I looked walking through the airport with that crew. I'm surprised airport security didn't stop them and ask where they were taking me. We hadn't even picked up my bags when they told me we had a few "stops" to make. "Do you want some swag?" they asked. Swag? Free stuff? Uh … yeah!

For the next couple of hours, we went on a tour of their sponsors. First, the guys took me to Etnies' headquarters, where we met a team manager at the door. "We're going on a trip tomorrow," one of the guys told him. "We need all new stuff. Head to toe." The manager hooked us up. I had never gotten so much free stuff in my life. I was used to getting free bikes, and even a T-shirt and shorts now and then from No Fear, my clothing sponsor. But anything I got was directly related to riding a motorcycle. This was different. They were throwing all kinds of gear my way.

We left Etnies around two in the afternoon and met up with another member of the Crusty crew, a guy they called Cartoon Man. His real name was Rusty. He was a terrible rider, but he would crash anything anywhere, so he made for good video footage. I kept looking around, thinking, "What did I get myself into?" Rusty drove us to the home of the owner of another of the Crusty sponsors in Huntington Beach. We pulled up to this enormous mansion. I can't imagine what the neighbors thought when they saw us standing at the front

THIS FANCY SETUP WAS
BASE CAMP DURING
OUR FILMING TRIP TO
THE CALIFORNIA
DESERT. NO CELL
PHONES. NO
TELEVISION. JUST A
LOT OF ROOM TO RIDE.

door. The owner came to the door dressed in a robe and invited us inside.

We walked in and there were girls everywhere, wearing nothing but panties and bras—and most of them looked like they had just woken up. The entire house was a cloud of smoke. "Hiiii!" the girls said as we walked in. My friends back home were not going to believe the day I was having. I was so overwhelmed; I don't think I said a word the entire time.

The owner, whose name I never got, sat down on his couch and started smoking out of a giant bong. Of course, at the time, I had no idea what it was. I remember thinking, "Why does the house smell so bad?" After a few good puffs, he brought us into another room and started stuffing our bags full of sunglasses and stickers. "Good luck!" he yelled as we pulled out of the driveway. "Have fun!" I put those stickers everywhere. That guy was cool. Then, we drove to the desert.

I'm pretty sure the guys would have taken good care of me. But they didn't have to. Instead, Micky Dymond, one of the most talented riders ever, drove out to meet us. Micky was 31 and at the peak of his career. A few years earlier, Micky was as crazy and reckless as any of the Crusty

THE FILM THAT LAUNCHED MY FREESTYLE CAREER

guys. Actually, he'd probably put them to shame. He loved to party and would have been a great freestyle rider. He was doing 180s and 360s on a motorcycle off hills and natural terrain before freestyle became a sport.

Micky was older than the other guys, and he had a wife and two young kids. He'd mellowed out a bit and was on this trip for one reason: to ride. For the next few days, he took me under his wing. The other guys would party all night and sleep late. Micky and I were up at six every day and we rode for hours before the rest of the crew woke up. On one of our morning rides, he told me about his dream to place a ramp at the edge of the Grand Canyon and jump his bike into the nothingness. He said most people thought his idea sounded crazy. I filed it near the top of my Do-Way-Before-I-Die list. It sounded like fun.

I had a great time on that trip. I definitely impressed the older guys. I was the guinea pig for every jump—the first one to go. They knew I wanted to make a name for myself and would do anything to prove I belonged. If anyone was going to get hurt, it would be me. If I didn't want to jump, they waited until I did. And of course, I always jumped. One of the jumps I test drove was a 160-footer. When I landed, I heard a thump that didn't sound like dirt, and the ground felt unstable. When I inspected the area, I discovered that I had landed on 200-foot-deep mineshaft covered with plywood. Then, about halfway through the four-day trip, I got busted.

It's one thing to get caught lying to your mother and be around to accept the consequences. But when you are in the middle of the desert with no means of communication, the consequences become much worse. My dad let it slip that I was in Los Angeles, and my mom realized I was with the Crusty crew. She finally got hold of Dana Nicholson, the videographer and co-founder of **Fleshwound Films**, and I don't know who was more scared—Dana or me.

Mom went ballistic. "Our son is never coming home," she said. "Those guys are going to kill him!" Dana told her he was taking good care of me. He told her that he had just had a baby and the whole crew had become much more mellow in the past year. My mom didn't believe any of it; she only knew their reputation.

Fleshwound Films (Flesh•wound•Films)

NOUN: An action-sports film company started in the 1990s by pro snowboarder Dana Nicholson and surf filmmaker Jon Freeman. After several snowboarding videos under the title *Creatures of Habit,* they released *Crusty Demons of Dirt,* their first motocross film, in 1995.

In the Pastrana house, it's not cool to say Yes when Mom had already said No. Dad was in the doghouse. Literally. I don't think he slept in the house until I got back. That happened sooner than I expected. I was shipped home after the fourth day—with a busted chin and a broken arm.

The final jump of the trip was called the Diving Board. It was going to be the "money shot" in the film. We knew it would be the most difficult jump so we saved it for last. No sense getting hurt before we finished the video. Before that shoot, the Crusty guys had taken a lot of riders to this jump—Jeremy McGrath, Phil Lawrence, Brian Deegan, Jimmy Button. Big names in motocross and super-tough guys. They all took practice runs and said, "No thanks." The take-off area was full of big whoops from riders changing their minds and braking. So you had to go through the whoops, and then clear a 100-foot gap with a 50-foot drop to a tiny landing.

You can imagine how badly it pissed everyone off when I cleared it on my first try. Rode away clean. Deegan heard I'd jumped it and was so mad that he drove up from another spot he was riding just so he could have a shot at it. He couldn't be outdone by a dorky kid who was nine years younger. Because my first jump was so easy, I started getting pretty confident. Over-confident. I jumped it a second time and tried to do a heel-clicker. I over-jumped, crashed on the landing, and broke my wrist. Dana duct-taped my arm, stitched up my chin with a needle and thread, and put me on a plane headed to Maryland. But not before I'd logged enough footage to create my first real video part.

That video was huge for me. The Crusty videos were popular worldwide and, until then, they'd only featured hardcore, tough-looking riders with tattoos and attitude. But they dedicated a full section to me. They showed video of me riding my first motorcycle, clips of me jumping at home, and tons of footage we shot in the desert. They edited my part to the song "Clean-Cut American Kid."

At this point, I was already a factory Suzuki rider and well-known on the amateur racing scene, but no one knew I could jump or do freestyle tricks. Thanks to that video, I became known as the freestyle guy. And for a while, to most people, that's all I was.

DAD SPEAKS

I was in the doghouse a lot—usually for good reasons. Debby felt strongly that Travis should not go to California, and I didn't blame her. Those guys were rough looking: shaved heads and piercings. But Travis really wanted to go, and I looked at as a once-in-a-lifetime opportunity. Before he left, I called Dana and said, "If this kid is exposed to anything— women, drugs, drinking —I am going to kill you. I'm not threatening you to scare you. I am serious. I will fly to California and I will kill you." He said, "Mr. Pastrana, that's fair."

Whoops (Woops)
NOUN: A.K.A. whoop-de-doos. A section of a motocross or supercross track featuring bumps in the terrain. The whoops are the toughest sections of most tracks.

A DOUBLES ROUTINE

Sometimes your greatest success is helping someone else succeed.

The best day of my life was the day I watched my friend crash on his head.

KENNY BARTRAM: Sure, best day of *your* life. What about me?

TRAVIS PASTRANA: Hang on, Kenny. Let me explain.

In March 1999, NBC announced a new action sports competition called the Gravity Games. It would be held in Providence, Rhode Island, a month after the X Games, and it would include a freestyle motocross event called Doubles. All of the riders had the same response: Doubles? We quickly got our answer from event officials: "Two riders, one course, one score." Cool. But I needed a partner.

I was only 15 and by far the youngest rider in the year-old sport, but I was one of the first competitors NBC invited. My good friend Kenny Bartram was not invited. Few people in the freestyle world had heard of Kenny, but I knew how good he was. Kenny and I met when I was 11 and he was 16. His uncle, Guy Cooper, introduced us at a motocross race. As soon as we met, Kenny and I started racing. We raced everywhere. We'd even race to a race. We have been great friends ever since we were kids and have spent a lot of time riding together at my place.

Naturally, I wanted Kenny as my partner. "Sorry," the organizers told me. "You have to pick a rider we've invited." That seemed like an easy fix. "Add him to the list," I said. "If you want me, invite Kenny." It took a bit of coaxing, but I convinced the Gravity Games to make room for one more rider.

KB: When I got to the event, you know the first thing the organizers said to me? "We had no intention of letting you into this event. You owe Travis. He's the only reason you're here." Thanks, NBC.

TP: Freestyle Doubles was an interesting concept. In 1999, freestyle was so new that guys were afraid to ride side-by-side. Metal ramps weren't created until 2001, so all the takeoffs were made of dirt, and the faces of all the takeoffs were full of ruts. The chances of something going wrong were pretty good, especially if another rider was trying to launch next to you. But Kenny and I didn't care. We wanted to put on a show. It sounds

Gravity Games (Grav•i•ty Games)

NOUN: An action sports competition held from 1999 to 2005 and broadcast on NBC and OLN.
Over the years, the event was held in Providence, Rhode Island, Cleveland, and Philadelphia.

MY FOAM PIT IS THE MOST POPULAR STOP IN THE NEIGHBORHOOD. KIDS LOVE TO WATCH US TRAIN. AND SOMETIMES, I TAKE THEM FOR THE RIDE OF THEIR LIVES. WITH THEIR MOM'S PERMISSION, OF COURSE.

I'M CREDITED WITH INVENTING THE LA-Z-BOY. BUT THE CREDIT SHOULD GO TO MY MOM. SHE EVEN NAMED IT!

corny now, but we choreographed our entire run. By the time we got to Providence, it was perfection.

Well, almost.

Kenny flew out to my place in Maryland two weeks before the contest so we could practice on my freestyle course. Kenny's one of my favorite people to ride with, but he's afraid to ride with me—especially before a contest. He used to work on a new trick for two months and figure out all the bugs. Then he would come to my place, get all excited, and immediately throw his new trick in front of me. I'd see it once, hop on my bike, and land it perfectly. He would get so annoyed. Making up a trick is tough. You have to figure out ramp angles and distance and weight distribution and, most important, you have to commit. But the second I see something, I can do it. Pretty soon, he stopped showing me his new tricks. I had to wait 'til the contest like everyone else.

KB: Dammit, Travis! I worked hard on that trick!

TP: Sorry, Kenny. That week, I worked with Kenny on a few new tricks and on our competition run. After a few days, we had it choreographed with all the big tricks: Can cans. La-Z-Boys. Whips. Those were big tricks in 1999. But we still needed a finale, a big finish that would leave the crowd

**THE CLASSIC WHIP—
AN OLDIE, BUT GOODIE.**

and the judges with smiles on their faces. I've always been the one with big ideas. Kenny's the pessimist who tells me my ideas won't work, or that he's not willing to give them a try. This time, Kenny outdid me.

His idea? To launch over a jump, side by side, and land on the same bike. He'd jump on the right, do a no-footed can, and hook his right foot onto my right foot peg. Then he'd grab onto me, ditch his bike midair, and we'd land with him sitting on the back of my bike. "I know we can do it!" he kept yelling. All I could picture was a Kenny Missile sailing through the air and tackling me—and both of us crashing. This time, I chickened out. "Okay, Kenny," I said. "Smaller finale."

KB: I was pretty sure I'd get hurt, but I was young and didn't care. Travis was afraid of what would happen to him. It's a rare day that Travis Pastrana turns down a challenge. I don't think he liked that the trick was out of his control.

TP: We were still trying to figure out a finale two days before we had to leave for Rhode Island. I started to think Kenny's idea wasn't such a bad one. Then, the perfect idea came to me. Backflips off the bikes. "We launch the bikes, do a flip off the back, and land on our feet," I said to Kenny. "How cool will that be?" No response. Kenny had never tried to flip off anything before, let alone a moving dirt bike. "Let's teach you to flip," I said. For the next two days, instead of riding, instead of working on freestyle tricks, I tried to teach Kenny a backflip.

Situations like this are my specialty; people just seem to push themselves further around me. Their confidence level rises. I don't know if they're trying to impress me, or if they don't want to be the guy who doesn't go for it, knowing I will. Or maybe they just need someone to tell them they can do it. But I'm going to push their limits, push them beyond the point they think they can go. If I say, "Okay, you're ready to backflip," then I have complete confidence they can do it. That confidence is contagious. I've "inspired" more than 100 guys and two girls to try backflips for the first time. Would they do that at home, without me there to push them? I'm not sure.

I'm motivated differently. I don't need anyone to push me because I have ways to push myself. For example, if you put a dollar on the table and say, "Go jump off that bridge because I just did," will I do it? Yep, every time. And I'll probably double backflip on the way down. If I have a vice, it's gambling. Not traditional Vegas gambling. Betting. If you want me to do something crazy, bet me a dollar I won't do it. Even better, do it first. Then bet me.

My dad decided to help me teach Kenny. We started on the diving board with a nice, soft landing. That didn't go so well. We had Kenny stand with his back to the pool, take a few bounces, then jump. But he flopped all over the place. He flailed around, landing on his head, landing on his back. Kenny is the opposite of a cat. He never lands on his feet. All day long—flop, flop, flop.

KB: I had such bad form. I never got close to doing a flip. I inhaled water every time I landed.

TP: The diving board was a lost cause, so we moved to the trampoline in my yard. It's bolted down flush with the ground and the dirt is dug out underneath. If you fly off, you don't have far to fall. But Kenny flew off in a different direction every time he tried. He landed on his head so many times that I can't believe he didn't break his neck. My dad didn't make it any easier on him.

Most of my friends know my dad can be quite a pain in the ass. If he thinks you're wimping out of something, he'll let you know. Loudly. So there's Kenny, trying as hard as he can, and my dad, the ex-Marine, is in

SAYS WHO?

This letters page ran in a 2002 issue of *Motocross Action* magazine. I cut it out, framed it, and hung it in my basement gym. When I need extra motivation, I read a couple of letters. Does the trick every time.

OUT OF FOCUS

What is Travis Pastrana's problem? He's not well enough to race, but he can do circus tricks on a bike? I think his focus is in the wrong spot.

–LOUIS WISE

LOOKING BACK

Travis Pastrana's most recent injuries in a long string of most recent injuries prove to me that he will never live up to the potential we saw back in 2000. He had one season in the sun, I enjoyed it and I wish him well. But I fear that he will never ride like the Travis Pastrana we once knew.

–PAUL NASH

PURPOSE IN LIFE

I spend every cent I make on motocross. I train, I practice, and I'm still not very good. If I had an iota of Travis' natural talent, I would think of it as a blessing. But raw talent is no good without a purpose in life. Travis doesn't have one, except to be noticed. And in case he hasn't been paying attention, people are noticing that he's stupid.

–KENT LAWLER

THE VILLAGE IDIOT

Well, it has finally happened. Travis Pastrana has finally managed to promote himself from factory rider to village idiot. Just exactly what does this kid want to do with his life? When you sign a contract, your employer expects you to live up to your end of the bargain. When this does not happen, your employer has just wasted a lot of money. If Travis is not committed to racing, then he should give that spot to someone who really wants it. Someone who shows up to race, not someone who has way too much other stuff on their mind. Someone focused on winning. Kyle Lewis, Nick Wey, Heath Voss, or maybe, hmm, I don't know, Guy Cooper. Air Time Cooper has left a profound impression on me this year. He's 40 and still kicking it on the track. I can't believe Suzuki hasn't already fired Pastrana. What a waste of natural talent.

–JAMES CHAPMAN

WE'VE HEARD OF TWITCH

Let's see if I've got this straight. There's a teenager from Maryland who has the physical attributes and speed to stand on the same hallowed steps as DeCoster, Hannah, DiStefano, Johnson, and McGrath. But instead, he wants to stand next to Twitch, Itch, and Stitch, with their cutoff pants and spider web tattoos. Am I missing something?

–MIKE FOLSUM

REQUIEM FOR A MIDDLE WEIGHT

In my opinion, Travis Pastrana is a victim of abuse. When he was being knocked unconscious at every race last year, a responsible person should have stepped forward to protect his delicate brain tissue from permanent damage. Even in the corrupt world of pro boxing, they are smart enough to throw in the towel before the fighter is reduced to a stumblebum. I think that each concussion led to the next and each crash had roots back to the first one. The AMA, the teams, his parents, and the people who cheered him on when they should have been asking him to heal up are guilty.

–STEPHEN BURNS

TWO CENTS WORTH

I just want to put in my two cents worth. Am I the only MX fan out there appalled by the stupidity exhibited by Travis Pastrana? Make a decision and decide if you want to be a racer or a freestyler. It's not refreshing, youthful exuberance anymore. It's just plain irritating. If I was Roger DeCoster, I'd can him.

–PAUL ARLT

THE FIRST STEP TO LEARNING A NEW TRICK—TEST IT OUT ON THE TRAMPOLINE.

his face. "Kenny! You can't flip! You freakin' wimp! You're hopeless!" By the end of the second day, Kenny was sore and tired, and he could only make it three-quarters of the way around. "Don't worry, dude," he told me. "I can do it. It's the final jump. I'll be fine." I sure hoped so.

KB: I wish I could defend myself, but I can't. It's all true. I was terrified. I'd never done a backflip. Travis' dad just shook his head every time I tried. Even after all that practice, I still sucked.

TP: At the Gravity Games, the freestyle singles event was first, so I didn't start thinking about doubles until after my run. Kenny was really nervous, and I knew he was thinking about the flip during his entire singles run. I won the individual event and Kenny took seventh. Afterward, everyone was asking, "Who is that guy? He's good." That event put Kenny on the map.

Before doubles started, Kenny and I met in the riders' area and talked through our run again, just to make sure we had every jump memorized. The TV cameras caught us and it sounded like we were choreographing a dance routine. As soon as we knew what trick we were doing over every hit, we relaxed. We stood at the top of the roll-in and watched the other guys. We weren't inspired.

By about the third run, the crowd had grown bored, even though they were watching the best riders in the sport: Brian Deegan, Carey Hart, Ronnie Faisst. But they were jumping on opposite sides of the course or crisscrossing over a few jumps. No one was riding side by side. Faisst and his partner staged a ninja-style fight in the middle of the course. It was cool, but it wasn't freestyle. A few guys rode follow-the-leader style, but they kept a lot of distance between them and did different tricks. Nothing was choreographed. In the end, doubles only lasted one year because NBC had trouble making it look interesting on TV. We were the only team the cameras could follow. Every other team needed two cameras, one on each rider. It was terrible TV. Most of the scores were in the 60s and 70s and the crowd didn't stand to cheer for a single run. Then it was our turn.

KB: Before we went out, Travis told me, "Go fast. Race the course." It was how he rode, still does. He said, "If you're having fun, it will excite the crowd. And if the crowd is excited, the judges will be excited. And if the judges have a smile on their faces, they'll give a better score." Damn good advice. Travis is the king of winning over judges.

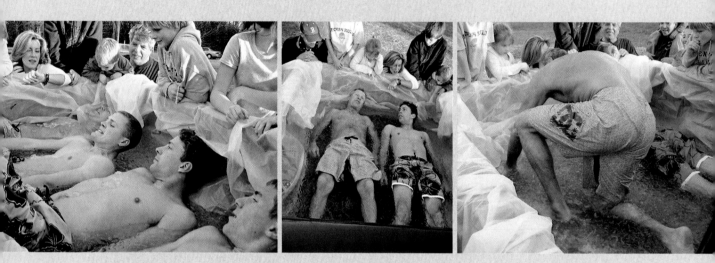

A COLD-BLOODED FAMILY

One Thanksgiving, my dad's family—all 50 of us—gathered at my grandma's house for our annual food-and-games-and-more-food fest. Around noon, I was in the front yard talking with my cousins about injuries. My cousin Daren Pastrana, who was the quarterback of his high school football team, had a sprained ankle at the time and was soaking his foot in ice water.

"Hey, Travis," he said, "how long do you think you could keep your foot in this bucket?"

"Until I decided to take it out—a long time."

"Do you think you could put your whole leg in here?"

"I could soak my whole body in ice water."

"No way. How long?"

"As long as I wanted to. Longer than you."

"No way."

"Want to bet?"

That's how it started. The next thing you know, my dad and I were driving a pickup truck around to the back of grandma's house. We filled the truck bed with water and all the ice from the industrial-sized ice machine she keeps in the garage. Then we pulled it into the front yard. My two cousins, my dad, and I stripped down to our boxers and climbed into the ice bath. And the clock started.

My cousins were the first to get out, after about three minutes, leaving just my dad and me. The two of us were on our backs for about two more minutes before my dad stood up and challenged me. "Okay," he said, "turn over." My family was standing around the truck, cheering us on as we flipped to our stomachs. After about three more minutes, my dad looked at me again.

"How long are you going to stay in here, Travis?"

"How long are you going to stay in?"

"Five minutes."

"Then I'll be here for six."

A few seconds later, I followed my dad out of the truck—$1 richer.

When it was our turn, I was trying to keep up with that 15-year-old kid, so I rode faster than I did in any motocross race. I was so focused on keeping up with him that I wasn't worrying about the run. The tricks just flowed. Until that final flip.

TP: Kenny and I didn't have a chance to practice together on the course, so we didn't know if we would have enough room to jump side by side, but we did it anyway. On a few jumps, we were so close in the air that we touched bikes and bounced off of each other. On one jump, we did no-footed can-cans in opposite directions, and our feet touched in the air. Coming around the next corner, I wasn't sure how close behind me Kenny was, so I slowed and accidentally stuffed him into the corner. Over that jump, I did a Hart attack and he did a bar hop. When he came over the bars, he was so close he grabbed my outstretched left foot. That was choreographed. When we landed, he hit my rear fender. That was not.

The crowd was on its feet for our entire run. On the final jump, we came in from opposite sides and did La-Z-Boys as we crossed. The takeoff was totally blind, so we just jumped and hoped we didn't crash into each other. We landed and came around to face this vertical wall of dirt. I looked at Kenny and nodded my head. Underneath the helmet, he knew I was smiling. That's the spot where we had planned to do the flips.

KB: When it came to that moment, I could hear Travis, his dad, Robert, and his mom, Debby, loud and clear in my head. They were all saying, "No matter what, do not back out. You have to commit." I thought, "I'm going to die. But dammit, I'm going to commit."

TP: We stood on the foot pegs as we rode to the takeoff. When we neared the most vertical section of the takeoff wall, I let go of the handlebars, threw my hands in the air, dropped my head back, and jumped off the bike. As the bike launched over the jump, I flipped. I got tons of air, so while I was upside down, I looked to my right. Kenny was splayed out, about to crumple. I felt so bad, but, man, it was funny. I landed on my feet and looked over at Kenny. He was upside down because he had landed square on his head. I thought he'd broken his neck, but as soon as the thought entered my mind, he was up. I started jumping up and down, pumping my fists in the air. When Kenny realized he was okay, he started doing the same. I ran over and jumped to high-five him, but I missed his hand and smacked him in the helmet. Almost knocked him

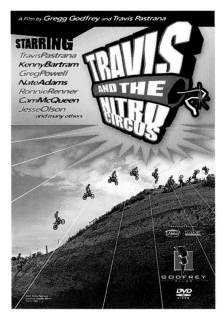

A Film by *Gregg Godfrey* and *Travis Pastrana*

STARRING
TravisPastrana
KennyBartram
GregPowell
NateAdams
RonnieRenner
CamMcQueen
JesseOlson
...and many others

TRAVIS AND THE NITRO CIRCUS

GODFREY FILMS

DVD VIDEO

back to the ground. It turned out Kenny compressed some vertebrae. But overall, he was all right.

KB: When I threw the bike, I lost all sense of where I was. I remember letting go, "flipping"—and landing on my head. I paused for a second, my neck all crinkled, and I looked over. There's Travis. Standing on his feet. Damn Pastrana.

TP: For that run, we earned the highest score in Gravity Games history—a 99.8. The only judge who didn't score us a perfect 10 was Kenny's uncle, Guy. He was so embarrassed that his nephew had landed on his head that he couldn't bring himself to give us a 10. Didn't matter. We still won.

The athletes I respect are the ones who go for it. The guys who step up and huck themselves because the vibe feels right. Rodeo clowns, mascots, bull riders, Mat Hoffman, Danny Way. (That's probably the first time Mat and Danny shared a sentence with a rodeo clown.)

That afternoon, Kenny was one of those athletes. My friend stepped up beyond anything he had ever done. For me, giving a chance to a guy no one else believed in, and then watching him step up, was incredible. He knew he couldn't flip, but he went for it. We won the gold medal. It was Kenny's first, and of all the medals I've won, it's my favorite. That was the best day of my life.

KB: Wow, thanks, Trav. I guess that was a pretty good day for me, too. It was almost three years before I tried my first flip on the bike. And you were there for that, too. Now, can I tell a quick story about you?

TP: Oh boy. Go ahead.

KB: After that experience, I started to think that riding comes too easy for this guy. In early 2000, I learned the truth. I invited Travis to Oklahoma to film a part for his movie *Revelation 199*. We went to a section of the Gloss Mountains that featured a bunch of tough hill climbs.

Travis had just moved up to the 125 division and he was still small for the bike. He struggled all day. I couldn't believe it. You never see Travis struggle. It was nice to find out that he works hard to develop his skills. In fact, he works harder than any other rider. He just doesn't let you see it.

TP: Okay, that wasn't so bad. Everyone has always assumed I'm a slacker.

They see this label that says "freestyle rider" and they think I don't care, don't work. And I've played that up. I remember watching Shaun Palmer and liking his style. Palmer used to show up late to an event, pretend he rolled out of bed at noon, and say, "I think I'll ride today. I haven't snowboarded in years." Then he would win a World Cup. After the race, he would walk to the podium looking as if he's already hammered, grab the champagne, down the whole bottle, and say, "I'm so good, I can kick your ass without even trying." But it's all an act. He used to go to Florida and train with Ricky Carmichael, who works harder than any rider in motocross. Slackers don't work out with Ricky Carmichael. I always looked up to Palmer.

My racing career didn't turn out the way it was supposed to, the way other people thought it should. There are a lot of reasons why I didn't win every championship, but lack of preparation was never one of them. I sacrificed everything to be a racer. But in the end, I just wasn't always the fastest guy at the track. People blame my lack of success on freestyle. But it's not the case. In 2003, I put freestyle aside and trained like I was Carmichael. I was a machine. And that was my worst year ever in supercross. I got slower. I was burned out and bored. I stopped having fun, and my lap times got slower and slower.

Injuries also hurt my racing career. I wasn't slowed only by freestyle injuries, but because I had a hard time seeing the big picture. At races, I should have thought, "I just need to finish well and be healthy for the next race." But that's not me. I lined up in the start gate of every race thinking, "Screw it. I might have been slower in practice, but I am going to win." Then I'd crash and get hurt.

It's difficult to look at an entire season when all you want to think about is the race you're in right now. I never wanted to look back and say I rode for second place. My career suffered because I was obsessed with winning every race. But I wouldn't change a thing. And in the end, the people I care about most know how hard I've worked and how much racing means to me.

KB: Trust me. He works. Don't let the act fool you.

TP: Thanks, Kenny, but you're not getting the last word in this chapter.

KB: Wanna bet?

TP: Nice try.

BEHIND THE SCENES OF *NITRO CIRCUS I*

In 2002, I teamed up with producer and rider Gregg Godfrey to create the first *Travis & the Nitro Circus* video. We have since released four NC DVDs in which my friends and I perform stunts that no one should try at home.

The first scene of Nitro I is not pretty. In fact, that jumped changed my career.

We were at Castillo Ranch in central California in 2002 and there was this huge jump I wasn't sure about. I took a few pre-runs at it, and every time it felt wrong. I kept telling myself I wasn't going to do it. I hadn't been filming with Gregg Godfrey for long, but he had never seen me fail. He had complete confidence. My dad was there, and he knew if I was unsure, I shouldn't jump it. But Gregg kept on. "What could go wrong?" he asked.

I took a last pre-run at the jump. I kept telling myself not to jump it, but I got past the point of no return and was in the air before I knew what I was doing. I flew about 150 feet and bailed off the bike halfway. I landed on my feet so hard that when I hit, I bounced and did a front flip. I felt my right knee explode. I ripped the cartilage and hit my femur and tibia so hard there are divots in the bones. "Woo hoo!" I yelled. "I'm alive!"

What people don't know about that crash is that it took me a full season to recover. For the first time in my life, I was 100 percent healthy headed into a race season, and in the best shape of my life. From that day, I've had to drain my knee every time I ride my bike.

MAKING A SPLASH

Damn the consequences—
you may only get one
chance to have the greatest
ride of your life.

When I was 11 or 12, there was only one television program that could keep my ADHD butt glued to the couch for more than five minutes: the **Summer X Games**. Reruns, wrap-up shows, pre-shows—didn't matter. Especially BMX Park. Dave Mirra. Dennis McCoy. TJ Lavin. I didn't miss a single run. Now that I know those guys personally, I'm an even bigger fan. BMX riders are the toughest guys in sports. Period. In comparison, freestylers are wimps. I thought being a part of the X Games would be awesome. But it would never happen for me because motocross wasn't part of the event. Until the summer of 1999, when I was 15.

When the call came, I couldn't believe it. ESPN was adding freestyle motocross to the San Francisco X Games, and I was invited. This was huge for our sport, and it was my biggest opportunity in freestyle yet. The only problem was, the event was going to be held the last weekend in June, the same weekend as the Mammoth Mountain Motocross race. Bummer.

Mammoth was going to be my first race against the top pros. It was important for my career and for my sponsors that I do well because I was in the middle of negotiating my pro contracts (which I would eventually sign in October). But it was also important to me to be in the X Games.

The folks in the racing world didn't know anything about the X Games. And if they did, they didn't care. Racing and freestyle are different worlds, and race fans don't have any respect for freestyle riders. Racers have incredible work ethics, train like maniacs, and ride to win. They don't care about creativity. Freestylers are generally lazy. They ride to have fun and don't care about winning. They see themselves as artists who ride for the feeling of accomplishment. A freestyler will cheer for his competitors. He'll finish fifth but be happy because he rode his best. Freestylers are inventors, motivated to be the first to try a trick. A racer is motivated by the guy in front of him. My sponsors had a hard time understanding my drive to risk my career—and my body—for freestyle.

Basically, this was not the time to start testing the loyalty of my sponsors. Because of my recent history with freestyle, they gave me an ultimatum: freestyle or racing. "And quite frankly," they told me, "you'll never make a living with those jumping shenanigans. Your career is in

Summer X Games (Sum•mer•X•Games)

NOUN: An ESPN-owned action sports competition held from 1995 to the present.
Freestyle motocross was also a part of the Winter X Games from 2000 until 2006.

racing, and you're risking it with this foolishness." It was hard to argue, knowing I'd spent the past nine months in a wheelchair recovering from a crash at a jumping contest called the Lake Havasu Free Air Festival (more on this later). I worked my ass off in rehab to get back to doing the things I loved. And I loved both—racing and freestyle.

My sponsors tried to convince my mom that the X Games were too big a risk. "We've all sacrificed a lot," she said. "You can't just give up on racing." And it's true: My parents did sacrifice a lot for my racing career, but they have always given me a say in decisions. Even when I was young, they respected the idea that if I wasn't happy doing something, it wasn't worth doing. If I wanted to throw away my racing career, it was my decision.

We sat down as a family and talked through the decision. My mom cried a lot. My dad tried to side with my mom, yet persuade her to see my point of view. Mom thought I was going to throw away my career on a stupid extracurricular activity. Back then, no one thought you could make money in freestyle. But my parents could see how important this invitation was to me, so we compromised. The Mammoth race was the day before the X Games, so we would go to the race. If I did well, we would drive through the night to San Francisco for the X Games.

The first part of the plan went well. We made it to Mammoth, but I had the worst event of my life. My foot peg broke on a huge downhill section and I crashed out of the race. I was bruised from head to toe. So much for

TOUGH ENOUGH?

Mat Hoffman is one of my heroes, and they don't come much tougher than Mat. But at the first Dew Tour contest of 2006, I found out the BMX guys are even tougher than I'd imagined.

I was in the medical tent on the first day of the contest, draining my knee for the first time that day, when Allan Cooke walked in. He had crashed during his first run of BMX Park finals, busted his teeth, broke his hand, and had a concussion. "Doc, fix me up," he said. "I gotta get back out there." There were 10 guys in the final, so he had about 20 minutes before his second run. He couldn't drink water because his broken teeth hurt too much. He was spitting blood, and one eye was swollen shut. The medic gave him an injection for pain in his hand, an IV for fluid, oxygen to speed healing. Allan lay down and fell asleep. Fifteen minutes later, he woke up and headed back to the course.

Meanwhile, Dave Mirra came in. He had knocked himself out and had no idea where he was. Head injuries tend to make you mean, so Dave was cursing and screaming and trying to convince the doctors to let him take a second run. Obviously, they turned him down. Minutes later, Ryan Guettler landed on his face and knocked himself out in warm-ups. His face was a mess and his vision was blurred. The docs loaded him into an ambulance, but 100 feet down the road he woke up, opened the door, jumped out, yanked the IV out of his arm, grabbed his bike, and headed back out.

And he won.

MOM SPEAKS

People think Travis is a showoff. But that's the thing about Travis. He would have done this jump if no one was watching. He usually prefers it that way.

impressing my sponsors. Still, my parents knew I had given my best, so we packed the van and headed to San Francisco. If everything went well there, we would make it in time for the riders' meeting.

The van we were driving had already overheated several times on the drive from Maryland to Mammoth, California. Now that we were pushing it through the mountains, it began overheating much worse. As we were driving up a steep section of the Sierra Nevadas, the alternator went out and the engine caught fire. We were only an hour into the eight-hour drive. My dad was frustrated. My mom saw it as a sign. "We shouldn't go," she said. "He's going to get hurt. We should go home." My dad tried to calm her: "If we get to the contest and the course looks scary, we'll go home." I could tell he didn't believe a word he was saying. But it didn't matter. The van was broken down in an empty park along the highway and it didn't look like we would make it anyway.

It was now one in the morning and we still had a seven-hour drive ahead of us. "Go to sleep," Dad told me. "We'll get you there." Eventually, my dad got the electrical problems sorted out and the van back on the road. Then, halfway up the east side of the mountains, the battery died. My mom was certain this was another sign. "It just isn't meant to be," she said. But Dad was not giving up.

My bikes and gear were stowed in the back of the van, along with a small generator. Dad fished out the generator, hooked it up to the battery with jumper cables, and fastened it to the motor with duct tape and straps. That generator provided enough juice to run the battery, but not enough to power the lights or the AC. Now we were driving up a windy mountain road with only the moon to light our way. Every 20 to 30 minutes, the generator ran out of power and the battery died, and we had to wait 40 minutes for it to recharge. At some point during all of this, I fell asleep, and when I woke up at six in the morning, we were parked on the side of the highway. My mom was still asleep in the passenger seat but my dad was gone. "Mom," I said, waking her up. "Where's Dad?" She told me he'd hitchhiked into town to rent a van. "He'll be back any minute," she said. I went back to sleep.

Dad returned about an hour later with a rental. We moved what we needed from our truck into the new van and by eight in the morning we were back on the road.

We made it to San Francisco, but I missed the riders' meeting and practice. Needless to say, ESPN was not happy. I could only imagine the conversations taking place as I rolled up less than an hour before the start of the contest.

"We invite the hotshot 15-year-old racer and he's too good to make it to the meetings? We'll know better next time."

I didn't tell anyone why we missed the meeting. I just apologized, grabbed my bike and gear, and headed to the freestyle course. Practice had already started, so I checked out the course while I waited my turn. The course was built on a pier along the San Francisco Bay and the setup was cool. From the bleachers, it looked as though you would land in the bay if you overshot the landing on a few of the jumps. The layout got the wheels spinning in the heads of all the riders.

"I bet you can make it into the water from that berm."

Berm (Burm)
NOUN: A banked turn on a racetrack or freestyle course.

"No way, it's too far."

"It's not too far, but the water's not deep enough."

"It's definitely deep enough. But you'd wreck your bike."

The water jump was the buzz in the rider area all day, but it was just talk. No one would actually give up their run—and their bike—for a dip in the bay. You didn't get extra points for pulling goofball stunts and our bikes weren't exactly cheap. By contest time, the bigwigs at ESPN knew we were talking about the potential for a little extra fun, so they called us together and told us ESPN would not be happy if someone "happened" to go into the water. To tell you the truth, that sounded more like a challenge than a threat.

When it was time for my first run of the finals, I was so excited that we had made it to the event that I had the performance of my life. Superman. Heel clicker. No-handed landers. No-handed seat grab. My first-run score was a 99.0, still the highest in the history of freestyle motocross at the X Games. The other riders pulled out all the stops trying to beat me. In those early days, everyone had similar tricks, so to win you had to play to the crowd. Mad Mike Jones stopped halfway through his run, put on a blindfold, and threw a whip off the center ramp. At the end of the round, the second-highest score was in the low 90s. I was pretty sure my second run would be a victory lap. That's when I started planning.

I had been riding for Fox Racing for years, and I knew that a few of the guys, including owner Pete Fox, were on a boat in the bay. Before my run, I called the boat over to the pier. "I want to backflip into the bay," I said. This was more than three years before anyone would try a backflip into a foam pit or on dirt, but I thought I could figure it out on the fly. I'd done plenty of flips on BMX bikes. A bit reluctantly, Pete agreed. "Let's get you some gear," he said. He borrowed a life vest from a wakeboarder who was in the boat with him, and I went around a corner where no one could see me and slipped it on under my jersey. One of the ESPN cameramen saw me and asked what I was up to. I confessed, so he turned the camera on and followed me for the rest of the day. "This will make a great show," he said.

I talked through the jump with my dad but decided to keep my mom in the dark, for her own good. I knew she was already in the stands biting her fingernails. Besides being my first major freestyle contest, I was riding the bike I had crashed at the Lake Havasu contest less than a year earlier. I knew thoughts of that accident were floating through her mind. I didn't blame her.

It was tough even for me to forget the Lake Havasu crash. I showed up at that event and started hitting the jumps without even looking at the course. I was hitting every jump better than the last. My timing was perfect, so I became over-confident. One of the jumps was a 120-footer, which no one was hitting. I thought, "I'll hit it. Won't even warm up. I'm that good." That's the last thing I remember. In videos, you see me take off, and as soon as my wheels leave the ground you hear my dad yell, "Oh, f—-!" Then I crash into the face of the jump and crumple to the ground, my leg twisted around the bike's handlebars and my body lifeless.

The next thing you hear is my mom scream.

I was unconscious, but I didn't hit my head and knock myself out; I passed out from the pain. It took nearly a week, countless tests, and one miracle doctor to diagnose my injuries. I remember very little of that week, but I still remember the pain. Any time the doctors moved me from the backboard to the MRI or X-ray machines, I woke up screaming. Then I would pass out again, which was my body's way of protecting me from the pain. It was horrible. Now I know that was my pain threshold, the maximum pain my body could handle. I'll never feel anything worse.

WHY #199?

No matter whether I'm riding freestyle, racing Supercross, or driving rally, I'm known as #199. But why the high digit? When I was younger, I was a huge fan of Robbie Reynard, who selected his first number, 593, based on the month and year he turned pro—May 1993. So I decided to do the same. The problem? A race number can only have three digits, and I turned pro in October 1999, or 1099. Easy fix. I dropped the zero. But I didn't realize it actually means January 1999. Oh well.

I was unconscious most of the time I was in the hospital, waking up just long enough to scream or tell the doctors where it hurt. I'd broken a lot of bones in past crashes, felt so many types of pain, but this was different. I felt disconnected, like I wasn't attached to myself, and the slightest touch to my abdomen caused intense pain. My mom said I kept asking, "Did anyone get it on film?" The X-rays showed no broken vertebrae, just several fractures of my pelvis and hips. But something else was wrong because those injuries alone would not cause such intense pain. My stomach kept growing bigger, though I had no internal organ damage, I wasn't eating, and I was receiving nutrition through an IV. Obviously, I was bleeding into my stomach and losing a lot of blood. But the doctors didn't seem too concerned. Then my dad met Dr. Wes Johnson, a spine specialist who had recently moved to Lake Havasu to treat jet ski riders. The world championships are in Lake Havasu and there had been a slew of back injuries around that time.

Dr. Johnson had been following my case and he was concerned. He walked into my hospital room and asked my parents to explain exactly how I'd landed. "Did he endo?" he asked my dad. Recognizing that Dr.

MOM SPEAKS

I knew something wasn't right. You know your kid. When the doctors said they couldn't find anything, I knew they were wrong. I fired two doctors, including the top guy. Then we were blessed. A new doctor had come to the area two months before. Without him, Travis would have died right there, while we listened to doctors tell us he was fine. I was strong when I had to be. After his surgery, I fell apart.

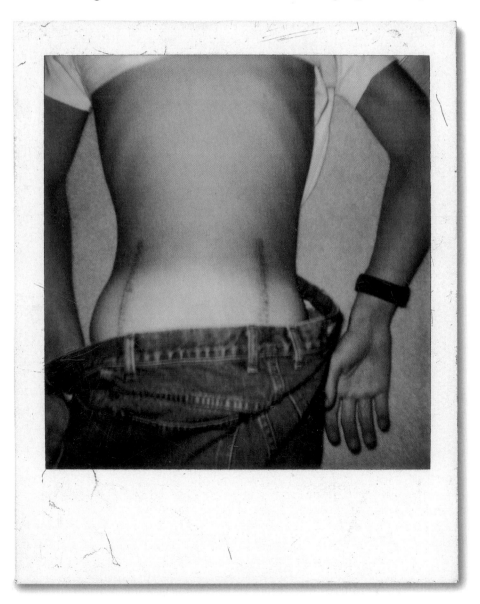

Johnson knew moto lingo, Dad pulled him aside and talked to him about my injury. Dr. Johnson asked my parents to tell the hospital to allow him to treat me. "Get rid of your current doctor," he said. "Your son is in a lot of danger." My mom immediately went to the doctor treating me and said in not-so-ladylike terms that he was fired. "You have two options," Dr. Johnson told them. "You can take him to a guy in Germany or to a guy in California. They're the only doctors qualified to perform the surgery he needs." Easy decision. The next morning, I was on a jet to a hospital in California for surgery with Dr. Joel Matta, a hip and spine specialist. Dr. Johnson had diagnosed me perfectly, even though my injury had only been documented twice before. One guy was paralyzed. The other didn't survive. I was damn lucky.

In simple terms, my spinal column had torn away from my pelvis. Lying down, it appeared everything was in order because no vertebrae were broken. But I couldn't move or sit up because my spine wasn't attached to the rest of me. In a six-hour surgery, Dr. Matta drilled holes in my hips and spine and inserted rods horizontally across my abdomen to fuse everything in place. I lost so much blood I received 10 transfusions. If

WHEN I RECOVERED FROM MY BACK INJURY, I GOT THE FASTEST WHEELCHAIR WE COULD FIND—AND PUSHED IT TO ITS LIMITS.

not for Dr. Johnson walking into my room that day, I wouldn't have survived the week.

The day after the surgery, Dr. Matta came to my room for a post-op checkup. He reached down and touched me on the shoulders. "Do you feel this?" he asked. "Of course," I said. He was stunned. From the moment I arrived at the hospital, he assumed I would be paralyzed for life. He never thought he was operating on a kid who would be back on his feet, completely healed, nine months later. "Think you would've done a better job in the operating room if you knew I wouldn't be paralyzed?" I asked, trying to lighten the mood.

I spent a week in the hospital and the next nine months in the fastest wheelchair available. I took that chair to its limits. I wheeled hundreds of miles around the neighborhood for training. I jumped it off dirt piles and raced my friends on their bikes. I didn't get back on a motorcycle until three months before the X Games, but thanks to my wheelchair antics, that was all the time I needed.

Waiting in the pits next to the X Games course, I was confident I'd won with my first run. I hated keeping my finale plans from my mom, but

DAD SPEAKS

I never stopped grinning that night, thinking about how far removed the ESPN officials were from what had just happened. He was having fun. I couldn't believe they made such a big deal. Travis spilled, at most, a half-gallon of gasoline into an already polluted bay. When I got into the room, Travis was nervous. He couldn't believe how many people they'd rounded up in less than 30 minutes—police officers, security guards, environmental guys. I kept reassuring him that they couldn't shoot him or lock him up. I told him to just answer their questions or let me answer them. We weren't told he wasn't getting his money until the next day when we went to pick up the check and found there was a hold on it. We should have gone home right after the contest.

when she knows about stuff like that beforehand, she gets so nervous. She loves being there for my big moments, though. My dad is the total opposite. He will do whatever it takes to make sure my equipment is in the best possible condition and that he's done everything he can to get me ready. Then he wants to be as far away as possible. He wants a call afterward to tell him how things went. Good or bad.

If I was still in the lead by the time my turn came around again, my plan was to hit the first jump, then ride toward the big berm. Instead of using it to turn, I would hit it like a launch ramp. I had to make sure I got enough distance to get out over the water, and enough rotation to flip all the way around and not get stuck under the bike. There were four guys in the Fox boat ready to pull me out of the bay in case I was knocked unconscious or pinned underwater by the bike. And, of course, my dad had a backup plan.

"If something goes wrong, just jump off the bike and I'll catch you."

"What?"

"I'll be underneath you, standing on the pier. Throw the bike. Land on me."

"Uh ... all right, dad."

He wasn't joking. He was prepared to catch all 185 pounds of me as I fell from the sky. In every photo, you can see him standing under me, head craned to the sky, hands outstretched. Thankfully, I didn't need his assistance.

When I got back to the rider area, the guys immediately noticed my new bulk. "What's up, Pastrana? You been working out?" I looked buff with that life jacket under my jersey. "I'm testing a new Fox chest protector, very revolutionary," I said. Everyone seemed to buy it. Because I had the highest score in the first round, I was the last to ride in the final round. When my turn came, I was still in the lead. Mike Cinqmars was second with a 97 and Brian Deegan was close behind with a 96.67. I had won the first freestyle motocross gold medal at the X Games. And I was pumped. My run would be a victory lap. Everyone expected me to goof over the jumps, have fun, put on a show.

When my name was announced, I tore onto the course, hit the first jump and landed solid. I then head toward the berm, rode straight up its side, and jumped nearly 100 feet away from the course. I could hear the silence of a confused crowd. "Where'd he go? What happened? What went wrong?" By the time anyone realized what I had done, I was sailing into the water.

The crowd went nuts.

The other guys couldn't believe I had done it. And man, it was fun. Now, about that backflip. I said it was my first attempt. It was more like my first semi-attempt. I was such a wimp. I pulled the handlebars, started to initiate a flip—then jumped away from the bike. I didn't commit. I tossed the bike away from me like it was on fire. My dad said when he saw me throw the bike, it looked like I was exorcising demons. Maybe I was.

As I fell through the air, I realized that the pier was nearly 30 feet above the water, so I had a nice, long fall. And the water in northern California is freezing. It felt like landing on ice-covered concrete. To top it off, the water was so nasty I had to get a tetanus shot the next day. The oil from my bike didn't help. But I paid for that. Literally.

The Fox guys picked me up in their boat but the bike sank so fast they weren't able to retrieve it. When we got close to shore, I jumped out and swam to the pier, grinning ear to ear. The crowd was going insane and I was having a blast. But when I got to the pier, two angry looking police officers and a very large ESPN executive were waiting for me. To a scrawny 15-year-old kid who had just pissed him off royally, he probably seemed even larger. He pulled me out of the water by the back of my life vest and looked me dead in the eyes.

"Son, wave at the crowd, look nice and smile. Because you just lost your gold medal."

"What? You can't take that away. I already won."

"You're damn right I'm taking it away. Stripping the medal. Now get your ass in that room."

"Yes, sir."

The three of them escorted me to a meeting room a short walk from the course. My dad was waiting there when we arrived.

"Son, you're going to jail!" The ESPN executive was still yelling at me.

"What for?"

"You could've shut down the X Games! Do you understand how serious this is?"

"Yes, sir."

Meanwhile, as I was being threatened with fines and jail time, my dad stood in the back of the room listening. And laughing. Not exactly the response Mr. ESPN was looking for. He stood up, turned red, and stared down my dad.

"Mr. Pastrana, do you think this is funny?"

"Well, you have to admit this is just a little funny."

"This is not a little funny! It's not funny at all. This is serious," he said, veins bulging from his neck. My dad was practically rolling on the ground laughing. "Your son is going to be punished. We're taking his winnings. All $10,000. And he's going to jail."

Long pause. "It's a little funny."

Honestly, I thought they were going to fight right there. I guess my dad and I see the world a little differently than most folks. For us, that day was about living in the moment. Those are the times I'm a lot like my dad.

Neither of my parents cares about winning and they never pushed me. I think my dad is the only motocross parent in history to stand on a track with the words "Slow down!" written on a pit board. Sure, my mom cares what people think about me, cares about consequences. But who else can say they launched their bike into the San Francisco Bay? No one. Yeah, it was a risk. We didn't have a dime at the time—we didn't even have a van to drive home. That $10,000 was important to us. My parents had taken out two mortgages on the house, sacrificed every penny for my career. There were times that my dad's brothers didn't take paychecks from the family construction company so we could buy fuel to go to races. But all the money in the world couldn't buy that experience.

When my father and I left the room, Todd Hicks from Fox spoke to the other ESPN executives and convinced them that since I won the event with my first run, I shouldn't lose my medal because of what I did on my second run. The stunt didn't influence the judges, so I should still be the gold medalist. ESPN agreed. But they still withheld my winnings to pay for the salvage of my bike and to clean up the bay.

The jump made national TV, and I got calls from people I didn't know I knew. David Letterman had me on his show later that year and showed the jump. Oddly, neither the jump nor the footage leading up to it ran on ESPN's broadcast of the X Games, and it was never featured in any *Best of the X Games* stories and shows. To this day, ESPN executives say the jump never happened.

On the other hand, my sponsors got great publicity out of the jump, and I became an X Games star overnight. Fox rewarded my "bad" behavior by giving me a $10,000 bonus to replace the contest money I'd lost. When I showed up to my first race as a signed pro a few months later, more people knew me from the X Games than from racing. It was going to be a good year.

MY WORLDS COLLIDE

Live every day exactly the way you want.

JAY LENO IS A BIG FAN OF MOTOCROSS AND HAS HAD ME ON THE SHOW A FEW TIMES. A COUPLE OF OTHER TIMES I WAS SCHEDULED TO APPEAR BUT HAD TO CANCEL. MY FRIENDS WANTED TO RIDE.

I couldn't wait to start racing after I signed my pro contract in October 1999. I was the happiest 16-year-old on the planet. My dad was the happiest 49-year-old. My parents had worked their butts off to get me to that day. Now I could afford to pay them back a little. With a pro contract came a mechanic to do all the work my dad had been doing and a manager and an agent to deal with the media requests my mom had been fielding. It also came with a lot of money, so my mom became much more involved. She's protective of me and wanted to make sure no one took advantage of my success.

My life in the months between winning the X Games in the summer and signing my contract in the fall was crazy. I got a ton of requests to be on TV shows, including Jay Leno and David Letterman. But at first I turned them all down. I planned to launch my pro racing career at the World Supercross at the Rose Bowl in Pasadena in November, so I had to do a lot of testing. I'm not much for the celebrity scene anyway. Red carpets? Not my thing. Those situations aren't fun for me. Now, give me a tractor and a wide-open field and I'm the happiest guy in Maryland.

I guess when it comes down to it, I'm just a walking contradiction. I want to be the center of attention (when I compete), but I hate to be the center of attention (on TV, in airports, at events). I'm extremely quiet and shy, but I can be the loudest guy in the room. I'm the most confident person in the world when I'm riding, but catch me on the dance floor with a girl and I'm a helpless dork.

Finally, in early November, I agreed to be on Letterman's show. I knew he wanted to talk about winning the X Games and jumping into the San Francisco Bay and would most likely ask me to perform a freestyle trick. The taping was on a Thursday in New York City, nine days before the race in Pasadena and less than 24 hours before I had to be in California to test with Team Suzuki. No problem. I was used to tight schedules.

As soon as I got to New York, I called my new team manager, Roger DeCoster. Appearances on late-night talk shows weren't prohibited in my contract, but I knew Suzuki wasn't going to be thrilled to see me on TV promoting freestyle. I didn't want to give Roger too much of a heads up, so I called him a few hours before the taping. "Hey, Roger! See you tonight," I said. I gave him my flight information and let him know when to pick me up at the airport. Then I dropped the bomb.

"I'm going to be on Letterman in a few hours. You should check it out tonight. I think it'll be cool."

"Letterman? Are you going to be riding?"

"Oh, no. Well, yeah. Maybe. They said they might have me do something."

"Something?"

"Nothing special, though. No big deal. Check it out."

That was a pretty scary conversation. I was supposed to inform Roger of everything I did. I probably should have *asked* him if I could be on the show, but the last thing I wanted was for him to turn on the TV and find out on his own.

Roger DeCoster is possibly the toughest man on the face of the earth. He's also one of the greatest motocross riders in history. He's from Belgium, a five-time world champion, and the first foreign-born rider in the Motorcycle Hall of Fame.

How tough is he? The legend is, in 1978, during practice before the World Championships, he was in a horrible crash. Hideous. He had so

ONE PLACE YOU'LL NEVER SEE ME: DANCING WITH THE STARS.

HOW TO UPSTAGE LEGENDS JEREMY MCGRATH AND TONY HAWK AT THE ESPN ACTION SPORTS & MUSIC AWARDS? TWO WORDS: BOW TIE.

DRIVE FAST.
SLOW DANCE.
By Nicole Mancuso

Travis and I met at the St. Louis Supercross race when we were 16. (I'm exactly one month older than him.) We've been good friends ever since. He pushes me to do things I would never do, like skydive for the first time. My senior year, I realized I was always doing crazy stuff with him, so I wanted to give him the chance to do something normal kids do. He was home schooled and never had a high school experience, so I asked him to my senior home-coming dance. I grew up in Naperville, Illinois, and went to Neuqua Valley High School. Travis flew in from Maryland that morning, and my dad and his friends took him to a local go-kart track for the day so I could get ready at home. Then he came back and got all decked out. It was fun to see each other dressed up, but he didn't know homecoming was much less formal than prom. He came out wearing tux pants. It was a pretty funny sight. I don't think most people know Travis is actually pretty dorky. If they didn't know, that outfit gave it away. So did his dancing! I admired the effort, but he was the worst dancer I'd ever seen. He was fine slow dancing, but when the music picked up, he looked gangly and uncoordinated. Hard to believe, right? He was doing the arm roll! In the end, we had a really fun time. I think he appreciated the experience, but I feel confident he would never do it again.

The City of Annapolis

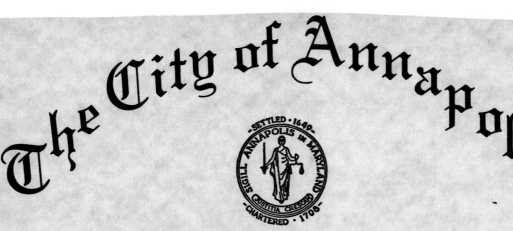

Mayor of the City of Annapolis to

Travis Pastrana, Greetings:

Be it Known: On June 29, 1999, as the youngest competitor in the event, you won the Gold Medal in Free-Style Motocross at the X-treme Games in San Francisco. This is the latest honor you have accrued over your eleven year national and international competitive career...and you are still only 15 years old. Other titles include: United States Amateur Motocross Champion, National Downhill Mountain Bike champion, International Under-16 Motocross Champion, and 13-time National Champion. In addition to your excellence in athletics, you are an outstanding student, having graduated from high school a full three years early and currently attending the University of Maryland, University College and Anne Arundel Community College, maintaining a perfect 4.0 grade point average. You have brought glory to yourself, your family and your community. On behalf of the citizens of this City, we salute you and confer upon you this well-deserved

Certificate of
Distinguished Citizenship

Given Under My Hand and the Great Seal of the City of Annapolis this 12th day of July, In the year of the Lord, One Thousand Nine Hundred and Ninety-Nine.

Mayor

much internal damage that the EMTs pronounced him dead on the track. On the way to the hospital, they revived him and treated him for a collapsed lung, broken ribs and a dislocated shoulder. Then he asked the doctors to tape him back together so he could race the following day.

They did—and he finished third. Needless to say, I did not want to piss a guy like that off. He didn't know me yet, and from what I'd heard, he was not a big fan. When everyone at Suzuki wanted to sign me, he said, "Hell no. I'm not having some sissy freestyler on my race team." Suzuki signed me anyway.

Back in New York, the Letterman folks had set up a jump on 53rd Street, right outside the studio near Times Square. I was fitted with a microphone so I could talk with Dave, who stayed behind in the studio. We chatted about the X Games and my jump into the bay, and I explained the difference between freestyle and racing. Then it was time to jump.

It was pretty cold outside and it had been raining all day. The landing ramp was made of wood, which I knew would be slippery. Not a big deal, though, because I was just doing a simple trick—a nac-nac. Dave gave me the cue and I took off. I hit the ramp perfectly, threw the trick, and landed squarely on the ramp. But my tires slid out and, before I knew it, I was on my side sliding along the pavement. I slid up the curb and smashed my shoulder into a fire hydrant. I hopped up, pulled it back into joint, and pretended everything was okay. "All good," I said, and gave Dave the thumbs up. I told the producers that the bike was too messed up to ride anymore. The truth? I was too messed up to ride. The bike was fine.

Once I was back inside the studio, I sat on the couch and chatted with Dave, pretending that nothing was wrong. In reality, my shoulder was killing me. I was hurt. But I couldn't let anyone know. Not Dave, not my parents, and especially not Roger. I smiled and goofed my way through that segment, then went

TRAIN MAN

My training has always teetered on maniacal, but in 2000 I trained so excessively that I contracted tonsillitis, chronic sinusitis, Espstein Barr, and parvo, and was forced to take a year off from racing. My sponsors were confused and worried about my physical condition, so they sent me to an athlete training facility in Austria for tests. The result: My VO2 max (how efficiently a person transports and uses oxygen) sucks. But my lactic acid tolerance and pain threshold are off the charts.

Translation: I'm not built to be a great endurance athlete, but I never "feel the burn" when I train or get sore the next day, so I work out too hard. I've never learned to recover, because I didn't know I had to.

Now I'm fully aware of my limitations, but routinely test my tolerance. In May 2006, I biked 200 miles just to see if I could, and I have a $1,000 standing offer for anyone who can beat my five-minute output on an archaic-looking rowing machine in my basement gym. I've passed out three times attempting to top my own record. I've only paid up twice, once to a photographer friend and once to my trainer, Todd Jacobs, who is a world-class triathlete. Damn guy still holds the record.

In June 2006, I bet motocross racer Ben Bostrom $1 that I could beat him through the swim and 112-mile bike leg of the Hawaii Ironman Triathlon. I've lost so many dollars to him. The guy makes $1 million a year, but he makes me sign every dollar he wins and then has them framed. Bostrom accepted the bet, so we asked our team manager at Red Bull if he could get us into the event.

The next morning, I drove to a local pool and swam 2.4-miles, then rode my road bike 112 miles around a 35-mile loop near my house. I can't run because my knees are wrecked from injuries and surgeries, so I set up my treadmill in the living room and walked for six and a half hours—until I finished a 26.2-mile marathon. By the end of my "triathlon," my legs were swollen, my feet were horribly blistered, and I'd lost several toenails. The next day, I called Red Bull. "Count me in," I said. Unfortunately, they couldn't get us entry spots in the Ironman. But it didn't matter. I knew I could beat Ben.

back to the hotel to rest. A couple of hours later, I remembered that I had told Roger to watch the show. That meant I had another scary phone call to make.

"Hello, you've reached Roger DeCoster..." I got his voicemail. Perfect.

"Hey, Roger. It's Travis! I just wanted to let you know my flight's on time. Also, I had a little incident this afternoon. Very minor. See you soon."

Then I flew to Los Angeles.

Roger picked me up at the airport and he did not look happy. "Little incident? No big deal?" he said in a thick accent. "Yeah. It's fine. Doesn't even hurt," I lied. "It looks bad," he said. "You can barely carry your suitcase."

"No way," I told him. "My shoulder's fine."

"Okay," he said. "Raise your arms. Both of them."

Uh oh.

It hurt so bad I couldn't do it. "I'll be fine," I said, knowing I had eight days to recover before the race.

I knew he didn't believe me. He said if my shoulder was fine, then I shouldn't have a problem waking up at six the next morning to go for a run with him. I called my dad that night and asked him what I should do. "You know what you have to do," he said. "You got yourself into this."

The next morning, I woke up at five. I was determined to make a good impression. Unfortunately, I don't run. Never have. But there were no bicycles, so running was the only option. And that old man could run. We ran four miles that morning. By about the third mile, my asthma had kicked in and I was wheezing like crazy. My shoulder ached. I was sweating, coughing, and choking. Roger hadn't even broken a sweat. So about a half-mile from the house, he looked at me. "Wanna race?" he asked. I smiled. "Beat ya there!" I said. I took off running as hard as I could, and I beat him. He didn't say it at the time, but I knew he was impressed. I was exhausted and in even more pain. Time to head to the track for testing.

My first laps were awful. My shoulder was so weak and I was in so much pain, I couldn't handle the bike through the whoops and I couldn't hit the bigger jumps. I was worthless. "Just go ride the hills. Try and get warmed up," Roger said. So I left the track and headed to the closest hill, a couple of hundred yards away. About halfway up a pretty vertical wall, I hit a rock with my front tire and got a flat. The hill was so steep, I couldn't hang onto the bike or walk it to the bottom, so I hopped off and slid the hill on my butt. I let go of the bike and it flipped nearly 100 yards down the hill and crashed into the ground below. The rims were shattered, the handlebars were smashed, the subframe was bent—the whole bike was a mess.

I had destroyed a $75,000 motorcycle.

I walked back down the hill to meet my team. "Where's the bike?" Roger asked. I pointed to a heap of metal lying at the bottom of the hill. "It doesn't run anymore," I said. I had never seen a group of men so pissed off in my life. "We asked you to warm up! How the hell did you wreck a bike warming up?" They'd had enough. "We're taking you to the doctor."

At that moment, arguing would not have been a good idea. "You have a second-degree separation and a torn rotator cuff," the doctor said after examining me. "We should get you into surgery." No way. I was not missing that race. "I'm fine," I told him. I looked at Roger. "Don't worry. I'm going to race this weekend. And I'm going to win." He thought I was crazy. "Pastrana, you couldn't win healthy," he said, "let alone with a dislocated shoulder." Maybe he was right, but I wanted to prove him wrong.

"I'm calling your father," he said. My dad and Roger are actually a lot alike, although Roger didn't know it back then. He told my dad he was impressed that I had gotten up that morning and was surprised to find out I wasn't a lazy freestyler. But he wasn't going to let me race with my shoulder as bad as it was.

"Did he say he can ride?" my dad asked.

"Yes. But the doctor said he should have the surgery. He can't ride a lap around the track. No way he can race."

"If he says he can go, he can go. The kid is tough. Let him race."

"Okay, then," Roger said, "I've been there."

My dad and Roger were finally speaking the same language. Roger understood tough. I left the hospital with some painkillers and called my doctor in Maryland to schedule surgery when I returned home. Then I took a couple of days to rest. By race day, I could barely lift my arm and I was in so much pain that nothing I took helped. I met with the team doctor, but all he could do was try to dull the pain. That's when I learned the secret of DMSO (dimethyl sulfoxide), a topical substance that seeps through your skin. On the day of the race, the event medics rubbed a little on my shoulder. If you put it on alone, it warms up your joint. But the medics mixed it with a box of crushed painkillers, and the DMSO carried the painkiller directly to the injured spot, so within minutes I couldn't feel my shoulder. Without the DMSO, my shoulder wasn't functioning well, but the painkillers at least took my mind off my useless shoulder. But the effect doesn't last forever.

I found that out halfway through the race. Halfway through the race, I was tired, and I earned a bad reputation that day. I was riding so hard that I took out almost every rider on the track. I even ran off the course myself a couple times. Toward the end of the race, I remember looking up in the stands and thinking, "If one of those people has a gun and they give it to me right now, I will shoot myself." I felt that bad. I just wanted it to all end—the race, the pain, the day. So I raced harder and faster because getting to the finish would make it stop. And because I'd told Roger I could win.

With five laps to ride, I got into a battle with Ernesto Fonseca, the best 125cc rider in the world at the time. Ernesto and I were friends and had been racing each other for years. He dominated the circuit the year before, but I was not letting him beat me this time. For three laps, we were side by side. But on the second-to-last lap, I took the lead. Then Ernesto flipped in a whoops section and my lead was secure. I was so tired I almost didn't make it to the finish line. When I won, everyone was shocked. Especially Roger. "You are no lazy freestyler," he told me. I had earned his respect.

The irony in this whole situation? Had I not hurt myself on the Letterman show, I might not have won that race. Because of the injury, I knew I had to win and I did. During the 1999–2000 season, I rode through a lot more injuries. My shoulder gave me problems all year. I broke my thumb and my wrist, and later sprained the same thumb and wrist. I was in a cast three times.

Being hurt is my best motivation. You're not supposed to be out on the track, and you're sure as hell not supposed to win. Roger once told me that if I ever lost a race and said I had anything left at the finish, I would be fired on the spot. I never forgot that. I may not always be the fastest rider on the track, but it's never for lack of trying.

BY WINNING THE 1999
WORLD SUPERCROSS RACE,
I WON THE RESPECT OF
MY SUZUKI TEAM
MANAGER—AND RACING
LEGEND—ROGER DECOSTER.

THE GRAND PLUNGE

Today's limits shouldn't be tomorrow's.

MOM SPEAKS

Ever since he was very young, when Travis says he's going to do something, he does it. So I knew this day was coming. He's not a spur-of-the-moment guy, like people think. He's meticulous in his preparation. His father and I always make sure he has the best training and equipment. We don't encourage him, but we support him.

I spend a lot of time inside my own head. If you catch me daydreaming, it's safe to say an idea is brewing. When an idea sparks, it won't be extinguished until I pull it off. That's the story of my Grand Canyon jump.

Micky Dymond gave me the idea during my 1996 Crusty trip to California. I don't know if he remembers telling me about it, but I constantly thought about jumping my bike into the Grand Canyon until I turned 18, when I could finally make it happen. When I blew out my candles on October 8, 2001, guess what I wished for?

I had been filming with Greg Godfrey since I was a kid, and we've made about 10 videos together, including three editions of *Travis and the Nitro Circus*. I love filming with Greg because he loves to ride as much as I do, so his goal on film trips was to have as much fun as possible. Coincidentally, shortly before I turned 18, my longtime sponsor Ogio hired Greg to make a movie called *Global Addiction*. All of our previous movies had been done on shoestring budgets, so we were both excited about this opportunity. He called as soon as he signed on to the film. "Travis, I have a budget!" he said. "A good one." This was my chance.

I told Greg about my Grand Canyon aspirations. He was psyched. So was Ogio. Mike Pratt, the company's founder, even threw a little more money at the project. When I turned 18, I was finally able to skydive legally, so a week after my birthday I flew to Salt Lake City to begin training.

I don't think my parents believed they'd soon be standing at the edge of the Grand Canyon and watch their only child disappear over its edge. When I left for Salt Lake, they smiled and said, "Okay, Trav. Have fun! See you soon. Good luck with your cool stunt."

I do know that my Suzuki sponsors were not so keen on the idea, and they even asked me *not* to wear Suzuki gear or ride their bikes, which meant I had to buy my own for the jump. Suzuki was taking a huge risk by supporting a rider—their top racer, no less—who performed in freestyle contests. They were not going to back him while he risked his life for what seemed like a thrill jump. I wanted to support them anyway, so I wore my blue Suzuki jersey on the day of the jump.

Like most of the big events in my life, I wanted Kenny to experience the jump with me. Kenny had known about my Grand Canyon dream for years, and we thought it would be cool to do a side-by-side jump. He met me in Salt Lake, and we drove together to the skydiving center. We had no idea what to expect when we arrived at Skydive Utah. We just knew we had to learn to jump well enough to make a 1,600-foot plunge into a

IF YOU'RE WONDERING WHERE
MY PARACHUTE IS—THIS WAS A
TEST RUN.

canyon. Greg had started working on permits, a ramp and a film crew—
and he already had set the date. The jump was just three weeks away. That
made our training even more critical. When we pulled into the parking lot
at Skydive Utah no one was in sight, so we walked the grounds for a few
minutes before the owner, Jack Guthrie, dropped into our lives. Literally.

As we are walking toward what looked like a main office, a
jumper attached to the tiniest parachute I'd ever seen came flying
toward us at about 100mph. I normally jump with a 230-inch chute,
which is pretty common. He was using a 70, a chute so small that it
looked like he was holding a piece of notebook paper above his head.
The winds were so intense that we were told no one was allowed to
jump, so Jack had decided to test the weather for himself, just to see
how bad the winds really were. He was flying toward us no more than
10 feet off the ground, swerving between the mobile homes where most
of the skydiving instructors live. He slid toward us on one foot, then
stopped a few feet before crashing into us. Kenny and I looked at each
other. "That's our guy!"

LESSON ONE: DON'T LOOK DOWN

By Greg Powell

In the summer of 2004, my cousin Travis called me up and asked me to go skydiving. I'd never done it because it's way too expensive. He said, "I'll cover you. Pay me back some day if you can." I jumped on my motorcycle and drove to the site to meet him. When I got there, he told me I was going to be jumping solo. I didn't know how he'd pull that off, but I also didn't think the idea of falling through the air with a big fat guy strapped to my back sounded like much fun. When the instructors asked to see our certification cards, Travis came up with this story about how I'd been out in Utah BASE-jumping with him a couple of years ago, but hadn't skydived in a while and I lost my card. The next thing you know, we're taking off in a plane with no paperwork. On the ground, Travis gave me the three-step approach to skydiving: strap up, jump, and pull the string. Easy. But once we got in the air, he started rambling on about all the infinite details you had to pay attention to or you would die. I couldn't remember any of it. I told him to stop and give me three things to remember. I went over his advice in my head, trying not to give away that I was nervous and inexperienced. When we got to 12,000 feet, we walked to the door of the plane. I looked down, looked at Travis and said, "Oh, wait. I have one more ques—." I didn't even finish my sentence. My cousin kicked me out of the plane.

For two weeks, Jack and his wife, Debbie, took Kenny and me under their wings. We lived at the drop zone and trained every day. Jack knew what my ultimate goal was, and he said most people would begin to transition to **BASE jumping** with about 100 skydives under their belt. I had two weeks, which meant a maximum of 40 jumps. "It's not going to work," he said. "You don't have enough time." But we had already set up the jump and I wasn't backing out. What's the difference between 40 and 100 jumps anyway? You just jump and pull the cord.

The first couple of days, Jack allowed us to jump only a few times. We spent a lot of time on the ground receiving instruction and I was getting antsy. And have I mentioned the planes? They were covered with duct tape and under constant repair by the mechanics. I was more nervous during takeoffs than when we actually stepped out of the plane. The fierce winds made takeoffs even more difficult, so I finally rented a helicopter and a bigger plane so we could go up more frequently. The instructors were psyched because they'd never had so much cool equipment to work with. We were all pumped.

Everyone, that is, except Kenny. We were a week into our training and Kenny hadn't progressed a lick. (Sound familiar?) Every time he jumped, he flipped through the air like tumbleweed before stabilizing himself. On a sky dive, you have plenty of time to get to your stomach and pull the cord. In the Grand Canyon, you have just 10 seconds before you hit the bottom, so you need to pull the cord in eight. If you're on your back and deploy the chute, it wraps around you. If you're spinning when you pull, you get line twist. In the Grand Canyon, either scenario means you're dead. Every time Kenny jumped, he'd flail until the five-second mark and stabilize himself by second seven or so. He was horrible. He never got to his stomach in less than seven seconds. Jack decided that Kenny should not try the stunt. I think Kenny was glad the decision came from someone else.

After two weeks of training, I needed to learn short-fall skydiving, or BASE jumping. We said goodbye to Jack and Debbie and rolled out of Utah. Next stop: the jump site in Hellhole Bend,

BASE jumping (Base•jump•ing)

NOUN: The sport of jumping from fixed objects (such as mountains) with a parachute.
BASE is an acronym for Buildings, Antenna, Span, and Earth.

THERE'S NOTHING TOUGH ABOUT A PURPLE, HIGH-WATER SKYDIVE SUIT. EXCEPT GETTING IN AND OUT OF IT.

Arizona. Kenny and I met with Greg and a bunch of riders to film for a few days along the way. The road trip was a blast, even though a lot of guys got hurt. Chuck Carothers knocked himself out and spent a few days in the hospital. Mike Jones suffered a concussion. Andy Bell also crashed and landed in the ER.

When I arrived in Arizona, I had only two days to train, so I needed the best BASE-jump trainer I could find. One name rolled off the tongue of every person I asked: Dave Barlia. He's the guy in that Suzuki commercial who guy says goodbye to his wife, walks out of his house, puts on a helmet, dives off the side of a cliff, and gets into his Grand Vitara. He's also a huge fan of motocross and was happy to help me. But he was not excited about the circumstances. "I've never trained anyone who has less than 400 skydive jumps," he told me. "I don't think this is a good idea. I'm only packing your chute because I am a big fan and I know you'll do it with or without me." He said he'd never been so scared in his life. I wasn't scared at all.

Once again, we started on the ground with instruction. Then I jumped from a helicopter several times. The first time, Dave jumped and I watched. Next, we jumped together. He explained that I would jump from the chopper and tumble for five seconds, then get my body face down and horizontal to the ground, just like skydiving. Then pull the chute. "Not bad," he said after our first jump together. But no matter how well I did jumping from the helicopter, Dave was still nervous. He wasn't convinced my training would be sufficient if something went wrong on the actual jump. "This is stupid," he kept saying. Sometimes I would overhear him say it under his breath. To be honest, I didn't understand what I was supposed to be afraid of.

In my opinion, I've always been good at recognizing and justifying my fear and equally as good managing it. To me, just because something is difficult or seemingly dangerous doesn't mean it's scary. A well-planned stunt like the Grand Canyon jump is no more dangerous to me than jumping off a high dive would be for someone like Kenny. Compared to other challenges in my life, this didn't seem so difficult. I had eight seconds to figure out how to get to my stomach and pull a cord. I had done my research, done the preparation, and hired the best people to train me and pack my chute. Obviously, the consequences of failure were much greater than usual. But even if I crashed to the hard ground, I figured there would be no pain. So what's to fear?

I seemed to be the only person with this point of view. I understood

MY MOM AND I MOMENTS BEFORE I JUMPED INTO THE GRAND CANYON (OPPOSITE). NOW THERE'S A MOMENT FEW SONS HAVE CAPTURED ON FILM.

I DREAMED ABOUT JUMPING MY BIKE INTO THE GRAND CANYON FOR YEARS. WHEN I LOOK AT THESE PHOTOS, I STILL CAN'T BELIEVE I HAD THE OPPORTUNITY TO DO IT. TWICE.

MOM SPEAKS

He had gone out of my sight, so I didn't see the parachute open. It took a lot longer than I expected. I was hyperventilating. I was yelling. I closed my eyes. I thought, "If that parachute doesn't open, I'm jumping in after him." No question. I was ready to go with him.

I MIGHT HAVE WALKED AWAY, BUT MY BIKE WASN'T SO LUCKY. WE HAD TO AIRLIFT ITS TWISTED REMAINS OUT OF THE CANYON.

AFTER I LANDED THE FIRST JUMP INTO THE CANYON, I COULDN'T WAIT TO GET BACK TO THE TOP AND SEE MY FAMILY AND FRIENDS—AND TRY IT AGAIN.

OF THE THREE PEOPLE IN THIS PHOTO (THAT'S MY DAD ON THE LEFT, AND BASE-JUMPING GOD DAVE BARLIA ON THE RIGHT), WHO DO YOU THINK BELIEVES THIS JUMP IS A GOOD IDEA?

Dave's fear. Aside from not wanting to see me splattered on the Canyon floor, his ass was on the line if anything went wrong. He's the one who packed a chute for an inexperienced kid. There's not another BASE jumper on the planet who would pack a chute for a someone with only 40 jumps, just so he could launch into the Grand Canyon. Dave knew me and he knew how seriously I had prepared. But the more he expressed his concern, the more everyone else became scared. Especially my mom. She thought I should call off the jump. Surprisingly, this time my dad agreed with her.

"Travis, I don't think you should do this," he said.

"Don't worry. I'm not nervous at all."

"I know," he said, "that's why I don't think you should do this. I don't think you understand the consequences. This is not a freestyle jump. If something goes wrong, that's it."

"I know, Dad. I'm not scared."

"Well, *I'm* scared as hell."

I tried calming my parents down, but as usual I didn't quite say the right things. "Don't worry," I told my mom. "If something goes wrong, I won't feel any pain when I hit the ground." Yet even though she didn't want me to jump, she let me know she'd be there beside me. She knew I wasn't backing down. The two days before the jump became really emotional. Me? I was only nervous about the bikes. We bought four used bikes for about $200 each, and they were in such horrible condition that I wasn't sure they'd make it over the ramp. I threw about 30 bucks worth of paint on them and covered them with stickers.

On the day of the jump, November 14, 2001, we built a wooden ramp at the edge of the canyon. Our process was about as unscientific as it gets. We eyeballed the placement of the ramp and cleared a 300-foot run-in so I could get enough speed to carry away from the cliffs. That was the most important part of the jump—making sure I had enough distance so I didn't drift back into the wall or land on the shelf about 1,000 feet down. I wanted to flip on the first jump, but my dad convinced me to use my first jump as a test. "If you don't make it around on the flip and get caught under that motorcycle, you're done," he said. "You have four bikes. Just do a few tricks on the first jump." I agreed. Then he made me promise. "I promise," I said. Dammit. Now I *had* to postpone the flip.

My mom took her spot alongside about 20 other folks lined up on both sides of the ramp. My dad would not get close to the edge. He's a softie when it comes to the moment of truth and likes to keep his mind occupied. During the X Games, he usually goes fishing to get as far from a TV as possible. My mom, on the other hand, was standing right at the edge. And she was a wreck.

Once the film crew was ready at the bottom and Greg gave the okay from the helicopter, I hopped on a bike and headed to the start of the run-in. I still wasn't nervous. But right before I took off, Dave, my BASE-jumping instructor, grabbed my shoulder and looked at me. In the nicest possible way, he said, "Travis, I think you're good. If you don't panic, you should be fine." Cool, I thought. "But if you do panic, you're going to die. Now go."

And with that, I took off.

I rode toward the edge, hit the ramp, and jumped into the canyon. I was fine on the takeoff, but as soon as I jumped, my heart sank because I couldn't see the landing. I never realized how much I looked for the ground when I jumped until it wasn't there. I freaked. I planned to do a decade air and a surfer, then jump away from the bike. But I forgot to do my tricks, forgot what tricks I had planned to do. I was so nervous that I

THE OTHER DA VINCI CODE
By Bob Burnquist

When I saw footage of Travis jumping into the Grand Canyon, I was amazed at how much fun it looked like he was having. I had my pilot's license at the time, but I hadn't sky-dived yet. Shortly after his jump, I started training.

For the next few years, I carried a mental image of Travis jumping into the Grand Canyon. When the opportunity came around for me to do a similar jump, I had more than 400 sky dives and a year's worth of BASE jumps under my belt. In the time since his jump, the mega ramp had debuted, Mat Hoffman had sky dived with his BMX bike, and Danny Way had jumped the Great Wall of China. I had a lot of inspiration to draw from. But Travis was my initial inspiration.

In 2006, I jumped into the Grand Canyon from the same location Travis had nearly five years earlier. The feeling of flying into the canyon was better than I'd dreamed. After that jump, I realized I really could do anything I set my mind to. I became addicted to the feeling of doing something new. You can't feel that excitement unless you do something new again. It's like Da Vinci said: "Once you have tasted flight, you will always walk the earth with your eyes turned skyward."

FOR PETE'S SAKE

I went BASE jumping one other time after the Grand Canyon. In 2004, I was in Austria for an event and decided to stay for a while to film with Kenny and Godfrey. After a few days, we were bored. We'd wrecked all the rental cars. I was still sponsored by SoBe, but I called Red Bull and asked if they could hook us up with parachutes and a spot to BASE jump. Their headquarters were nearby, and they sponsored BASE jumpers, so I figured they'd know who to call.

The next morning, they hooked us up with Stinky Pete. That was our nickname for him. He had one leg, smelled terrible, and spoke very little English. We thought someone was playing a joke on us. Nope. Pete was an expert BASE jumper and a friend of Felix Baumgartner, one of the best jumpers in the world. "Let's jump," he said.

The four of us drove as far as we could up the mountain, then got out to walk the rest of the way. I couldn't believe I was trusting my life to this guy. And I couldn't help wondering how he'd lost his leg.

Turned out, Pete had a BASE-jumping accident a few years earlier. His chute opened with line twist and spun him off course—a chute he had packed—and he broke his leg when he landed in a tree. I was nervous knowing he had packed our chutes and started to rethink the jump. But as the thought crossed my mind, I saw Pete standing at the edge of the cliff, looking down at the 3,000-foot drop. "Jump," he said. "Now." He wasn't going first. He wanted to watch me. I wasn't walking down, so I waited for Godfrey to turn on his camera, then I jumped.

started throwing random tricks, a can-can, a heel clicker, a nothing. Then the wind began to lift the front of the bike, so I jumped off to get away from it. Before I knew it, I was on my back, the one place I did not want to be, flailing my arms Kenny Bartram-style. "Whatever you do," I said to myself, "don't panic."

At five seconds, I felt resistance from the air and started to flip over. At six, I got to my stomach. At seven, I reached for the cord and at eight seconds, I pulled. I heard the bike smash into the ground about a second and a half later. When the chute opened, my body jolted as I instantly slowed from 130mph to 5.

I was alive.

And it was the scariest, most amazing thing I had ever done.

My mom was bawling when I got back to the top. She had seen me flailing and knew I shouldn't be on my back. It was impossible for her to tell how far I was from the ground, and she wasn't counting seconds like I was. She was just yelling, "Pull the chute! Pull the chute, Travis!" And she was a happy woman when she saw that red parachute open.

As we prepared for the second jump, I felt more confident. Time for the flip, I told the small crowd. "How cool is it going to be to take off, throw a flip, look back, and see nothing? Oblivion."

They all just stood there, staring.

"You are an idiot," was the most common response. My friends thought I'd lost my mind. I was surprised they didn't understand. Most were freestyle riders who did "crazy" stunts every day.

I had never landed a backflip on a motorcycle before that day. No one had. Carey Hart had tried one and I broke my foot attempting to figure it out the year before. But I figured it couldn't be too hard off this ramp. I was mentally prepared for the jump this time, and excited to try the flip. The second jump—the one most people saw in the video, on Jay Leno, and on news programs—went about as perfectly as it could have. I took off from the ramp and pulled as hard as I could on the bike. As I came around to the point where the nose of the bike was pointed straight at the ground, I was supposed to let go and get straight to my stomach. But the sight was absolutely beautiful, mesmerizing. I got so caught up in the moment that I almost forgot to jump off the bike and pull the cord.

Almost.

I watched the ground come at me for an extra second or so, then did a heel clicker and let go. I pulled the chute and floated to the ground. We had an extra camera on the ground filming the bike's plunge. It was humbling to watch footage of the bike explode as it crashed into a ledge above my landing spot. That could have been me.

After the jump, my dad pulled me aside. "I know we have two more bikes," he said. "And I know you can do it. But we can't take any more jumps. Your mom and I can't watch you do that again." So I stopped. I think everyone on that cliff breathed a sigh of relief when I told them I was done.

The next day, I got a call from Bob Burnquist. Word of my jump had spread and he was psyched. He wanted to know all about it—how I prepared, how long it took, how many cameramen I had with me. "I'm learning to skydive," he told me. "Sign me up for the sequel."

Five years later, on March 23, 2006, Bob duplicated my jump on a skateboard. Same location, same jump. Except Bob was more prepared. Over the preceding five years, he had become an amazing skydiver and spent a ton of time practicing in wind tunnels. I'm still terrible, and I've only BASE-jumped one other time, on a trip to Austria. I was honored that Bob wanted to repeat my jump.

I want to revisit the Grand Canyon jump in 2007 or 2008. It won't make my sponsors happy, but what they don't know …

Just kidding. I'll tell them—*after* I'm safely at the bottom. And this time, I want to launch off the ramp on a Harley at 120 miles an hour with a hot girl in a bikini on the back and me in a leather jacket on the front. Would that make a badass photo or what? I would love to jump with someone I know, but I couldn't live with myself if something went wrong. So instead, I need to find a female BASE jumper with a heck of a lot more experience than I have. "SWM seeks attractive, BASE-jumping F to take the ultimate plunge."

I wonder if there are web sites for that.

FULL CIRCLE

Sometimes the biggest risk is not taking one.

I f one thing sets freestyle motocross apart from other sports, it's injuries. It's not how often we're injured. Or even how badly. It's our ability to compete at the highest level once the damage has been done: broken bones, torn ligaments, concussions. As long as you can bend your knees enough to get your feet to the pegs, and you have at least one good arm, you can ride. Trust me. I've tested this theory with dislocated shoulders and torn knees. I've ridden minutes after suffering a concussion, three days after surgery to pin and plate a compound fracture, and with broken bones held in place with duct tape. There's always a magical fix that will get you through a two-minute freestyle run. And I know most of them.

Contest doctors are usually my willing accomplices. When I get to an event, I tell the medical staff about my injuries (most of them, anyway)

FILLING IN THE BLANKS

Because of concussions, there are several blank spots in my memory. The 2003 Gravity Games in Cleveland is one of those clean slates. Fortunately, I have friends to fill me in.

I wrecked in practice and dislocated my shoulder so badly I couldn't lift my arm. Tricks that required use of my shoulder were out, but without those tricks, I couldn't win. Before that day, I'd never lost a freestyle contest. But just as I was about to withdraw, I got the motivational speech of my life from Rob Van Winkle. Vanilla Ice.

Robbie comes to a lot of races. He's a big fan, and even used to race himself. He overheard me telling my friend Malcolm I didn't want to ride if I couldn't win.

"Travis, every time I sing *Ice, Ice Baby*, I can't win. But people love to hear me sing that song. A lot of people came because they love to see you ride. You see those kids? They came to see you perform. It doesn't matter if you can win. What matters is that you perform for them."

He was right. So I rode. And that was the first freestyle contest I ever lost. To make it worse, I also made a fool of myself on live TV.

Even with my shoulder in pain, I decided to try a trick that required use of my shoulder—a Superman seat-grab backflip. When I went for the trick, my shoulder

gave out, I missed the grab and … lights out. I don't remember anything after that. (Here's where friends, and videotapes, come in handy.)

I lay on the ground curled into a ball for about 10 seconds, then jumped up before the medics reached me. I waved at the crowd and pumped my fist in the air. The crowd cheered, so I ran to the bleachers, climbed into the crowd and started high-fiving people. The NBC crew thought I was fine, just having a good time. But my friends and family knew I was acting very strange. My mom began yelling to the cameramen, "He's not okay! Look at his eyes! Stop filming him!" But they stuck the microphone in my face anyway.

"What happened on that trick?" the reporter asked me

"What? I crashed?" I asked. "Was it bad? What trick was I doing? A 360?" I looked like an idiot, a deer in the headlights.

"No," he said. Now *he* looked confused. "You crashed on the Superman flip." Right. I knew that. "So what happened?" he asked.

I stared at him for a few seconds. I looked drunk. "Well, I guess I crashed."

They cut to commercial.

and what treatment I need in order to ride (cortisone shots, knees drained). Most of the doctors at events like the X Games or the Dew Tour understand that when a guy is crying with a broken bone, he's not crying out of pain. Pain is tolerable. He's crying out of frustration and desperation. If he doesn't compete, he's missing an opportunity. Competition is his livelihood. He needs a doctor who will fix him up well enough to get him back on the course without risk of further injury. The doctor's job is to give us the facts, tell us our options, and then support us in our decision, even if they disagree with it. Those are the doctors I like.

A week before the 2003 X Games, I blew out my left knee during practice. Knee injuries were nothing new to me. I'd already had six surgeries on my left knee alone. This time, I tore my ACL and LCL and had a partial tear to my PCL. Basically, my knee was floating around in there. I knew I needed surgery. I also knew surgery could wait until after the X Games. I had missed the 2002 X Games with a torn ACL in my right knee, and Mike Metzger dominated. It was hard to watch from the pits, and I couldn't miss the biggest event of the season for the second year in a row. For one thing, my sponsors were going to fire me. More than that, I wanted to show the world I was still around. I had a special trick planned for these X Games, one I had spent the entire year working on and one that no rider could possibly top. That's if I landed the trick. And to land it, I had to compete. And to compete, I had to postpone surgery.

But there was one small problem with that plan.

Running along the outside of your knee is your popliteal artery, which is an extension of your femoral artery. It carries blood from your heart to your upper and lower leg. With a complete ACL and LCL tear, there is very little keeping your knee from shifting to the side and severing that artery. "You have to immobilize your knee," said Dr. Tom Dennis, my local doctor, after he examined me on the day of the injury. "We'll brace it for now, but we need to get you into surgery immediately. Before then, don't do anything risky—especially riding." Hmmm. If anyone would have cleared me to ride, it would be Dr. Dennis. He'd been treating me since I was a kid, so he'd seen it all. Besides, Tom is a shoulder specialist. After visiting him, it was clear what I needed to do: get a second opinion.

The next morning, I flew to Indianapolis to see Dr. K. Donald Shelbourne. He ran the Shelbourne Clinic and was the team doctor for the Purdue football team. Dr. Shelbourne revolutionized the treatment of ACL injuries; he can get a football player with a torn ACL back on the field in three months. He's spent quite a few hours in the operating room with me. The X Games were in four days, so he was my last chance. "Hell no you can't ride," he told me. "I'll get you into surgery tomorrow. We'll get your knee fixed up and get you back 100 percent. You'll miss the X Games, but you'll be healed in a few months." Again, that's not what I wanted to hear. So I had to break the news to my parents.

I called my mom the next day. "Hey, Mom, doc says it's good to go. I just have to be careful." Then I went to the airport to catch a flight to Los Angeles. Unfortunately, my mom knows me too well. She wanted her own second opinion. First, she called Dr. Dennis. He didn't want to alarm her, so he sugarcoated things a bit. "Well, it's not what I recommended," he told her, "but he's an adult." She was skeptical, so she made another call. "Get your son off that plane!" Dr. Shelbourne said. "He cannot compete! If he severs that artery, he has between 10 and 30 minutes before he bleeds to death internally. If he crashes, he could die."

You can imagine how well Mom took that news.

When I got to the airport, I turned off my phone. It's rare that I answer it anyway, but I knew she would be calling. Amazingly, my phone never rang. Then, about five minutes after I got settled in my seat, a police officer and a man from airline security walked onto the plane.

"Travis Pastrana, please ring your call bell," came the announcement over the loudspeaker as the two men walked down the aisle, asking for each passenger's name. This could not be good.

Ding. I hit the bell. "Mr. Pastrana, please come with us. We've been told to escort you off the plane. Your mother called and there is an emergency at home."

"Oh, I'm sorry, officer," I said. "I just spoke with my mom. Everything's fine. If you don't mind, I'll stay right here."

"Your mom told us you would say that. Now please come with us."

"No, really. I just spoke with her. Right as you were walking on the plane, she called." He knew I was lying. But I continued. "Sir, I'm sorry. But I am not getting off this plane. I'm going to L.A."

"All right, son. I can't drag you off the plane. It's your decision."

So I flew to Los Angeles. Not surprisingly, my mom was on a plane right behind me.

Her persistence didn't stop once we got to L.A. From the time she landed, she was begging, pleading. She had never been so insistent that I not compete. She even tried appealing to my competitive side. "Travis, you don't like to lose," she said. "And you are going to lose. And quite frankly, no one is going to care that you're hurt. Your sponsors aren't

BEHIND THE SCENES OF *NITRO CIRCUS 2*

Black Wednesday. The worst day in *Nitro Circus* history. We were at the end of production for *Nitro 2* and didn't have enough footage, so I called every rider I knew and told them I was holding a video competition. Best footage from the day would win $4,000 cash.

SCENE ONE: My cousin Greg and I drove to a bridge not far from my house and parked in front of a popular restaurant. I got out of the car wearing a cowboy hat and no shirt, holding a shotgun loaded with blanks. Greg was wearing a black bag over his head and his hands were tied behind his back. I yanked him out of the car and "shot" him. Greg pretended to fall dead over the rail and belly flopped into the river, his hands still tied. Great footage—until the police showed up at my house (for the first time that day). The witnesses at the restaurant thought there'd been a real murder and 911 calls flooded the station.

SCENE TWO: As soon as the police left, I walked around to my foam pit—just in time to see a guy I'd never met launch a street bike *over* the pit and fall 25 feet to the concrete. The sound was horrendous. I thought the guy was dead. The kid's name was Street Bike Tommy, and he was alive but in a lot of pain. He crushed every bone from his waist down. Within minutes, the cops were back, joined by an ambulance and a medevac. As the medics loaded Tommy into the helicopter, a police officer started writing a ticket. Apparently, Tommy had wheelied his motorcycle past a police car earlier that day. He then took the police on a high-speed chase through Davidsonville. The same officer was called to the scene of his accident. Tommy was loaded into the helicopter holding a fistful of tickets. He's now one of my closest friends, and not much wiser from the experience.

SCENE THREE: During this chaos, a few guys drove my green ramp van to the street in front of my house. The van has ramps on the front and back, and BMX rider Colin Winkleman was going to jump over the van from the front ramp to the back ramp. Colin was to remain standing as the van drove straight at him at 18mph. But he took two pedals and got too much speed. He sailed up the ramp, over the van, and missed the landing and fell straight to the asphalt. He broke his back and both ankles and dislocated both wrists. Back came the police cars, an ambulance, and the medevac unit. My neighbors didn't know what to think. By the time the ambulance arrived, there was no pulse in one foot and Colin had to be airlifted to the same Annapolis hospital as Tommy.

At the end of the day, we had great footage and we split the prize money between Tommy and Colin, who were in the hospital. Unfortunately, it didn't even pay for their medevac flights.

"THE X GAMES IS ABOUT LANDING A TRICK THAT'S BIGGER AND BADDER AND GNARLIER THAN ANYONE THOUGHT POSSIBLE. THERE'S NO FEELING LIKE IT."

MOM SPEAKS

I have constant panic from the time Travis starts a freestyle run. It is an emotional roller coaster. I'm *on* that bike. I feel every jump. I tried to talk him out of doing the 360, but he was so passionate about that trick. I was scared. This wasn't just a broken leg. If he hit the wrong way, he would be crippled. When he went down on the first attempt, I knew he was hurt. When I saw he was going for a second, I was like, "No, no, no! Please, no." But he'd worked so hard I knew he had to try again. Travis loves his sport, and he loves his fans. When he landed that 360, I was so happy. Now get off the bike!

MEDICAL MYSTERIES

Some of my medical issues are easily explained with science. Others keep my doctors awake at night.

For instance, I hate to travel because I get horrible motion sickness. I fly every week of my life and get sick every time. I am a racecar driver, but I will throw up if I sit in the passenger seat of a car. I can backflip dirt bikes over 100-foot gaps, but I can't go upside down on a rollercoaster.

Also, I cannot wear sunglasses. I get horrible vertigo, get dizzy, and fall down. I can't make it up a curb wearing sunglasses. I'll trip or run into something. I don't even like wearing motocross goggles, but I have to.

Speaking of vision, a car crash corrected mine. I've had some crazy outcomes from concussions, but this was the most bizarre. In 2001, I crashed my Corvette and suffered a bad concussion. Before that, my vision was 20/25. Not so great. After, it was 20/15. Much better.

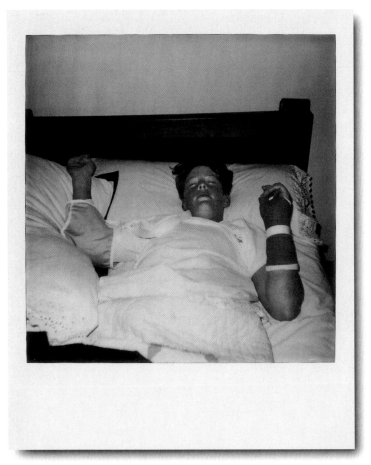

going to want to hear about a knee injury. Do you want to let everyone down?" The truth is, she was really worried. But come on, doctors always give you the worst-case scenario. And what were the chances of that? Besides, even if I did sever it, I had a few minutes. The doctors would take care of me. Mom continued to plead, so finally I called my dad in Annapolis. Surely he could talk some sense into her.

"Look, Travis," he said, "I've always stood behind you, no matter what you decide. But some day, your luck is going to run out. This could be that time." I didn't think so, and competing in this event was too important. Eventually, as always, my parents allowed me make my own decision. As always, they gave me their input, but once I made a decision, they supported me 100 percent. "I'm going to ride," I told my dad. "I'll be fine."

But I wasn't fine.

I had one day to practice and my knee was so swollen I couldn't move it. I had to throw out half my tricks because I couldn't use my right leg to hold me on the bike. I hadn't practiced my regular tricks all year because I'd spent all my time working on my one big trick. It was risky to try it with this injury, so I needed to learn a couple of new ones. And I needed somewhere to practice.

That night, the X Games held a kickoff party at the Playboy mansion. Sweet. What 19-year-old doesn't want to party with Hef and some Bunnies? Like an idiot, I skipped the party. Instead I called Carey Hart, who lived nearby, and asked him if I could borrow his foam pit for the evening. Although he was competing against me in best trick, he was gracious enough to say yes. He met me at his place, let me in, and turned on the lights. Then, in the middle of the night, on a torn-up knee, the day before the X Games, I taught myself a backflip heel clicker and flips off the distance ramps. My secret banger trick had disappeared, though. I completely forgot how to do it. But I thought I could win without it, especially with my new tricks.

When I got to the event the next day, I was nervous. My parents were nervous. Even Kenny was nervous. He was one of the few guys who knew about my new trick. He kept saying, "Dude, don't do it. It's not worth it." But he knew I couldn't work on a new trick for a year and then show up at the X Games and not give it a try. "You don't have to do it," he kept saying. "Save it for next year. You have a great run without it." The doctors were worried, too. "I'll be fine," I told them. I even lifted my pants leg to show off my specially designed knee brace. The brace was duct taped so tightly I could barely bend my leg. There was no way my knee was slipping out of place.

As I stood in the riders' area at the top of the roll-in, I started to get amped. The X Games had just moved west from Philly, and we were at the L.A. Coliseum. At night. The place was packed—40,000 people—and the crowd was intense. That's what I needed to take my mind off my knee. By the time Myles Richmond took the first run, I'd forgotten all about my injury. This was the X Games. Time to step up.

For me, the X Games is about more than just showing off. It's about working for a year to invent a trick that's bigger and badder and gnarlier than anybody thought was possible. To go out onto the biggest stage knowing your odds aren't great, and still going for it with complete confidence—there's no feeling like it.

Each rider had only one run in the finals, and I was the second-to-last guy to ride, based on scores from prelims. Nate Adams would ride last because he had the highest score. Nate is the most technically perfect rider in the sport, and he was going to pull out all the stops that night. Because Nate was following me, I needed to leave the judges with a run they would remember while they were scoring Nate.

Brian Deegan hit the course, and most of his run was average, at best. He wasn't throwing anything I couldn't beat. But after time ran out, he stayed on the course and started pumping up the crowd. They were psyched. They knew he had something else to show. I was interested to see what trick he would pull out now, after his run had ended. He rode back around to the final kicker, and the second his wheels left the ramp, my jaw dropped. Then the announcer confirmed what I thought I had just seen, "A 360! Brian Deegan lands the first 360!" I thought, "Well, damn. That son of a bitch stole my trick."

What were the chances? The 360 was the trick I had been working on for nearly a year. At the time, I had no idea that a video of my throwing the 360 into my foam pit had leaked onto the Internet (thanks to my room-mate, who had posted it for a friend). I thought, "How do two guys on opposite ends of the country come up with the same variation of the same trick at the same contest?" I couldn't believe it. "I should've just stayed home," I thought. Deegan came up a little short on the landing, so the trick wasn't perfect—it looked more like a 270 than a 360—but he muscled the bike around and rode away clean. The crowd was impressed. So was I. Deegan had only two weeks to study the video and learn it himself. Before that night, he said he had tried the 360 10 times into the foam pit—and landed it clean three times. Those are terrible odds, and he had never tried it on dirt. What he did was ballsy, but it

CLIFFHANGER

SUPER FLIP

THE TRICK LIST

The sport has evolved to my style. Every rider has put his flair into freestyle and developed it into what it is today. I was the first rider to bring several BMX tricks to motocross, including the Superman Backlip (or Super Flip) and The Nothing. I also invented more than 200 tricks on a motorcycle. A few highlights:

CLIFFHANGER: The first trick I invented, at 14. My mom named it. That first year, two guys in the world could do a cliffhanger. Now 14-year-old kids are doing double-grab rock solids.

LA-Z-BOY: My mom gets credit for inventing the La-Z-Boy. I started laying back on the seat and taking my feet off the foot pegs. "Mom, Check it out! I don't fall off!" My mom suggested I take my hands off and lay back more. She thought it would look cooler. "No way! That's not possible! The front end will drop away!" I said. But I tried anyway—and it worked.

FLINTSONE: This is a no-handed, no-footed trick where you "run" alongside the bike. The name speaks for itself.

RODEO: One of my less coordinated friends was jumping on the trampoline and told me he had an idea. He jumped, wadded up, and attempted to do a heel clicker variation. He didn't do what he wanted to, but the trick he was doing looked cool, like a one-handed heel-clicker. He named it the rodeo. Then I did it on a dirt bike.

BACKFLIP VARIATIONS: If there's a backflip variation, chances are I invented it. **SUPER FLIP, SUPER INDIAN FLIP, BARSPIN BACKFLIP** Everyone figured all backflips were the same. Not at all. Backflip combos opened a new avenue for inventing tricks. Being the first to do each one was fun because I had no idea what was going to happen the first time I tried them.

DOUBLE BACKFLIP: The best—and worst—thing that ever happened to me.

BACKFLIP CAN-CAN

sucked for me. Now there was no question that I had to throw the 360. To be honest, I wasn't excited about it, but Deegan forced my hand. That was all the motivation I needed. It was my turn.

Right out of the gate, I had the crowd on its feet. I rode down the roll-in and started by flipping the biggest gap on the course. At least I was the first guy to do something. Good thing I'd stayed up all night at Carey's place learning those long-distance flips. My entire run was a showcase of flips, any kind of flip. With my knee injury and lack of practice time, I didn't have much else. Except for the 360. Once I hit the course, my nerves were gone. I wasn't thinking about my knee or the consequences of crashing. I felt no pain. I raced around the course trying to excite the crowd because I knew I was not giving my best performance. But all that would change on the final jump. I made the turn at the far side of the course and rode toward the ramp directly in front of the judges' stand, the same jump Deegan had used for his 360. I had the crowd behind me. I

LA-Z FLIP

"EVERY DAY, I PUSH MYSELF TO REDEFINE THE LIMITS OF OUR SPORT."

couldn't lose. I hit the ramp perfectly and initiated the turn over my left shoulder while forcing my front wheel to stay down, level with the back wheel. I spun 360 degrees ... and crashed on the landing.

Before I knew what I was doing, I was back up. I grabbed my bike, got back on and waved off the judges. I put my finger in the air to signal "one more!" The crowd was going nuts. Time had expired while I was retrieving my bike, but I didn't care. It wasn't about a score anymore. I needed to land the 360. And all I knew was that I had crashed once and survived. Had Deegan not landed the trick, I might have called it a day. But he did, so I had to do it again. It wasn't until I was on my way up the ramp for the second time that reality hit. In those few brief seconds, I thought, "What are you doing?" I couldn't feel any pain at the time, but I was certain I was going to crash again. My knee brace had smashed on the first crash, so it was useless on the second jump. "I'm scared," I thought. But I gotta go for it.

As I hit the ramp, the jump felt right. This time, I spun the bike around and landed clean. I was pulling so hard I nearly fell off the back of the bike, but I stuck that trick. It might have taken me two tries, but I did it. You could have lit all the homes in Los Angeles with the energy in the arena. When my score came up on the screen, I was in first place.

I did not envy Nate Adams. Who would want to ride now, after all that excitement? He needed an incredible trick, but I knew the chances of that were not good. Nate's not the type of rider who creates tricks. Nate waits for someone else to invent it, then he does it better. Maybe this time he had something we didn't know about.

Nope. Nate put up an impressive run, as usual. His tricks were flawless; much better than Deegan's or mine. Nate is so calculated, so smooth, so technical. The crowd politely clapped after each trick, but it never really reacted, never had fun. Nate could dominate our sport if he would just realize that freestyle is about entertaining the crowd. It's about putting on a show. Nate might be having fun on the inside, but you can't tell. In my opinion, if you're not having fun, don't get into freestyle. If you want to win, take up racing, get to the checkered flag first. With freestyle, the crowd—and the judges—want to know you're having a blast.

Nate had the best run, by far, but he took second. I won. I couldn't believe I had even thought about not competing. I didn't win because I was better. I won because the crowd was pumped. I almost crashed my brains out on every trick and I kept the crowd on edge for the entire minute and a half. Watch the tapes. Deegan had a horrible run. He should have been dead last. But he stepped up and did a 360, so he got third. I had a horrible run, but stepped up, tried a 360, crashed, got up and tried it again. The judges took a lot of flak for the way they scored that event. Technically, they weren't allowed to count any of the 360s, since we landed them after time expired. But you'd be foolish to think our scores didn't reflect that trick.

And they should have. We want to put on the best show, so we push ourselves to redefine the limits of our sport. But inventing a trick is hard. You're doing something no one has ever done. You don't have a reference point to base your experience on, and you don't know if what you're attempting is even possible. It's a big investment, and a big risk. In the months it takes to learn a trick, there's a good chance you'll get hurt, like I did, and possibly take yourself out of competition for a while. And the second you land the trick in public, it's obsolete. Every rider can learn it in a couple weeks. The 360 was a particularly tough challenge.

The 360s that Deegan and I landed during freestyle finals were nearly identical, with the wheels flat, or parallel to the ground, all the way around. But in best trick finals the next day, Deegan threw another 360. This time, the bike was more vertical, so it looked more like an off-axis backflip or an inverted spin. At the time, not even the judges understood the difference between the two types of 360s.

After the contest, the announcers asked Deegan what he wanted to name the trick. "The Mulisha Twist," Deegan said. So from that point on, the inverted flip version of the 360 was known as the Mulisha Twist. The more difficult version, which both of us had thrown in the freestyle event, was called a flatspin 360.

Although the Mulisha Twist soon became a routine trick, no other rider attempted a flatspin 360 until the 2006 X Games. Ronnie Faisst had been practicing the trick into the foam pit at the **Metal Mulisha** compound in Temecula, California, and could land it every time—even on dirt. But during freestyle prelims, Faisst popped off the ramp a hair late, maybe 1/100 of a second, and didn't rotate. He spun about halfway around before he crashed to the ground, facing backward. He sprained every joint on his left side and knocked himself out of the contest. Still, he gets my respect. After all, if none of us ever went for it, we'd all still just be racing.

Metal Mulisha (me•tul•muh•lish•uh)

NOUN: A group of freestyle Motocross riders headed by 10-time X Games medalist Brian Deegan and including Ronnie Faisst, Jeremy "Twitch" Stenberg, and Jeff "Ox" Kargola, among others. The Mulisha riders live in Southern California and are known for their rowdy behavior, tattoos, and all-black gear.

FIRST TO TWO

Do great things—even if no one is watching.

The double backflip. As recently as 2004, the thought of completing two backflips on a dirt bike seemed impossible—or at least nuts. We'd only been doing single flips for two years, and a lot of guys weren't even comfortable with those. But by the summer of 2004, I was already starting to think about the double.

One afternoon that July, I was jumping into my foam pit, working on tricks with my cousin Greg Powell (we call him Special Greg) and my best friend, Jim DeChamp. They were jumping BMX bikes into the foam, throwing double flips and even triples. After landing a double on his BMX bike, Jim got a bright idea. "Trav, why don't *you* do a double?"

I thought about it for a second and decided there was only one way to find out if it could be done. "Get ready to pull me out!" I yelled. I was fairly certain I'd land upside down in the foam beneath a 250-pound dirt bike. And that's not somewhere I wanted to be for long.

The guys climbed up on top of the foam pit as I rode back to the top of the driveway. I turned the bike around and immediately blasted down the run-in, without giving myself time to think. For a first try, the result wasn't bad. I spun a little more than one and a half rotations before I landed upside down, buried in foam at the bottom of the pit. To get me and the bike out, Jim jumped into the pit and swung the arm of the homemade rope-and-pulley system into place. (Learning **freestyle** tricks is definitely a group effort.) As I was being lifted out of the pit, I thought, "This sucks. The double *is* possible."

I didn't have enough hangtime to complete two rotations, which meant I needed more height. We pulled the metal ramp back, from 45 feet to 60 feet, and I tried it again. This time, the ramp sent me so high that if I was doing any other trick, I would have sailed over the entire foam pit. But for the double, the height was perfect. I got all the way around on both flips, tires underneath me, and landed in the foam. "That's so cool," I thought. "It's going to work." Then I stopped and realized what I'd done. "Oh crap! It's going to work." I couldn't stop now.

The X Games were a month away, and I became dead set on doing the double in my freestyle run. I usually dedicate a couple of solid weeks to learning a new trick for the X Games. But this was going to take more time. A week into working on the double, I had Kicker, an audio components

Freestyle (free•stīle)

NOUN: A discipline of freestyle motocross. Riders perform a series of tricks on a course made of berms, ramps, and dirt jumps. Each run lasts 90 seconds and is scored by a panel of judges.

company and one of my sponsors, install an intercom system in my helmet, just like the ones NFL quarterbacks use to talk to their coaches. Jim had been doing doubles on BMX bikes for years, so I asked him to be my coach. He could watch my takeoff and know whether I was long or short, if I was under-rotating or over-rotating. Because I hadn't done many double flips, I still couldn't feel when something was wrong. And because I was spinning so fast, I couldn't spot the landing. From then on, every time I jumped, as soon as my tires left the lip of the ramp, I'd hear Jim say, "long," "short," or, if necessary, "bail."

By the time I got to the X Games in Los Angeles, I was not even close to landing the double consistently. But I still planned to do it in freestyle. I had never lost an X Games freestyle contest, and it was in freestyle that I had landed the 360 a year earlier.

I didn't tell anyone about my plans, but ESPN officials knew I was up to something when I asked for a few modifications to the ramp setup on the course. When I told them I wanted to try a double backflip, they immediately started hyping the trick. It became the buzz of the event. Unfortunately, during freestyle practice, I crashed trying a 360 and broke my wrist and ankle. I had a black eye that was swollen shut and a severe concussion. The medics pumped me full of painkillers, hooked me up to an IV, and taped my wrist and ankle so I could compete.

Once again, duct tape saved the day. But the double was out. So was the 360. I rode my best, but I lost to Nate Adams. Nate threw a 360 in his first run and I wasn't willing to attempt anything that risky. Losing was tough, but Nate deserved the win. And to be honest, that crash was a blessing in disguise.

I was scared to death going into that X Games. I put a lot of pressure on myself. And knowing what I know now, I don't think I could have landed the double, even if I had been 100 percent healthy. The ramp was too short and I had too little experience with the trick. I honestly believe I would have killed myself had I tried it. After the X Games, I tried to put the double out of my mind. But it was hard for my fans to let go of the trick. Everywhere I went, people asked, "When will you do a double backflip? Why didn't you do it at the X Games? Don't you want to do the double?"

BARSPIN CONTROL

The problem with the barspin back-flip? It looked too easy. But it was the most technical trick I'd dreamed up. Try to follow along.

First, I launched off the ramp and started the flip. Then I had to immediately hook one foot under the brake and one foot under the shifter, but be careful not to shift up a gear. (The special bike had no clutch and an automatic delayed-response throttle.) Then I hit the front brake, but not too hard, to stop the gyro effect of the front wheel. If I hadn't hit the front brake, I couldn't have thrown the handlebars as hard and they would never have made it around a full spin. Once I did hit the brake, my momentum completely stopped, so I had to restart the back-flip and get my body back far enough on the bike to throw the bars and not hit myself in the knees. Then I waited until the bars came all the way back around and then caught them again. Until I had the bars in my hands again, I couldn't do anything to speed up my rotation. Once I caught the bars, I was flying a dead stick, as I like to say, because the front end wasn't working. The tire wasn't spinning and there was no gyro. That means if the bike wasn't perfectly aligned with the landing, I wasn't landing the trick. If the bike was sideways, I was crash-landing sideways. There was no way to pull it back.

Got all that?

IT TAKES A VILLAGE TO BUILD
A STEP-UP JUMP FIT FOR A
DOUBLE BACKFLIP (OPPOSITE).

A HISTORY OF BRAIN BASHING

I've been knocked out on almost every continent, in every way possible. Since I was eight, I've had an average of two major concussions a year. When I was nine, I had a concussion that put me in ICU for four days.

I can deal with broken bones, but I hate the feeling of a concussion. They scare me more than any injury. They're unpredictable. For a few weeks after a concussion, I'm slow, lethargic, and my body shuts down. There's no telling how long that feeling will last. I have friends who have had dozens of concussions, but no lasting effects. And I have friends who were severely brain damaged by their first concussion. I can't live in fear of what might happen when I get on my bike. When my time's up, it's up.

In 2001, I was 17 and racing motocross. That year, I had three concussions in a row. I was leading the season by 50 points and I had to withdraw before the season ended. That was hard. I wanted to keep racing, but Suzuki, the AMA, and my parents convinced me to rest. My first concussion, at Southwick, wasn't so bad. It happened in practice. I was able to see straight by the first moto, so I got back on the bike and won the second moto. I was throwing up for a few days, but nothing too severe.

The second happened in New York. I led every lap of both motos and on the final lap, I was goofing a bit and crashed over a jump. I landed on my head and was out for a good 10 minutes. When I woke up, I was in the hospital eight hours later. Apparently, when I came to, I thought the race was still going on. I did a heel clicker over the big jump and a nac-nac over the final jump. Then I wheelied across the finish line as the 250s were waiting to start their race. The guy with the checkered flag said, "Son, you're 20 minutes late. The race is over." I rode to the pits and wandered aimlessly until someone found me and delivered me to my parents.

The third time, I landed right at my dad's feet. It was two weeks after the second concussion and I still couldn't hear well because of the ringing in my ears. When I got home, I could barely walk to the mailbox without blacking out. I threw up for days. After that one, I was done. I tried to ride out the season, but it wasn't possible. My parents and sponsors took a lot of flak for allowing me to continue as long as I did.

In 2006, my gray matter experienced another hat trick. I went to a Monster Truck event in St. Louis. I planned to compete in the world finals and needed practice. I'd never driven a monster truck on a real course, and now I had my own ride. The course was so much bigger than it looked on TV. I was scared out of my mind. For good reason. It didn't take me long to crash and smack the back of my head. Lights out. That was a bad concussion. I threw up for a week. But I planned to race the Daytona Supercross event the next week. I couldn't back out.

I was so lethargic from the concussion that I had a terrible race. Late in a heat race, I was coming through a huge whoops section and missed one. I flew over the handlebars and hit the back of my head, again, on the dirt. I staggered back to the bike but it was broken in two. I could barely see and my hearing was totally gone. I threw up five times a day for two weeks. I wasn't used to the effects lasting this long, so I went to my doctor for a CAT scan. The results were good. No hemorrhaging, but enough swelling in my brain to warrant time off. "After two concussions this close together," the doctor said, "you should take one year off. Another concussion in the next year could kill you." But I had a freestyle contest in Mexico the next week.

A couple of days later, I woke up feeling much better. And even better the next day, so I flew to Mexico— to support the other riders. Once I got there, I had to compete. I rode well. I won all of my heats and made it to the three-man final. Then, in the final round, I crashed hard trying to hit a box feature on the course. I flew straight to my head and was knocked out cold. The other riders freaked. They knew my doctor's orders. I was unconscious for almost five minutes. They thought I was dead. Gregg Godfrey ran down the stadium stairs so frantically that he tripped and broke his ankle. When I woke up, everyone was shocked. I was confused and groggy for a minute, and lost my vision completely for about an hour. But by the next morning, I felt better than I had in weeks. I never threw up again, and my energy returned the next day. The brain is a mystery. At least mine is.

THE RIDE OF MY LIFE (THAT NEVER WAS)

By Ryan Sheckler

I come from a Motocross family. My dad was a top amateur in his day and I've been riding for years. I met Travis at a Supercross race in 2003 and couldn't believe he knew who I was. We've been friends ever since.

I went to his house for the first time right after we met. I think he likes to show off when you're a newcomer. I knew it was a dangerous place, so I was scared. I didn't know what he had planned. The first day, he put me on the bike with him. I was on the front, near the gas tank, with my feet on top of his. I was in charge of braking and shifting. We started off mellow, but then he took me to his Supercross track. We were going over 75-foot triple jumps. I was shaking. That was the scariest thing I have ever done. The moment I got off the bike, I called everyone I knew.

At the X Games the next year, that ride gave him an idea. The bike he brought for the best trick contest broke, so he was out of tricks. He asked me to get on the bike with him again. He was going to backflip the big ramp with me along for the ride. I was down. I knew he'd get around, no matter what. And if not, I knew how to fall. I ran and got my gear. My mom almost flipped when she saw me putting it on. Unfortunately, the ESPN execs shut him down. They said they'd kick Travis out of the X Games for doing a tandem jump. It's probably good it never happened. But man, that would have been cool.

That fall, I tried to forget about the double. For the next year, I didn't practice it, or even think about. By the time the 2005 X Games rolled around, the double seemed so far away. Instead, I had been focusing on an idea I borrowed from BMX. I had a motorcycle built that would allow me to do a barspin in the middle of a backflip. I would let go of the handlebars, spin them 360 degrees, and grab them again—all while upside down in a backflip. The bike had the brake and throttle cables routed through the tubes so they didn't twist when I spun the handlebars. The barspin looked simple enough, but it was one of the most technically difficult tricks I'd ever dreamed up. Right before the X Games, some ESPN producers came out to my place in Annapolis to film segments for the TV broadcast. I was excited to show them the trick I was working on. But they didn't care about my trick or my bike. All they wanted to talk about was the double.

"Are you going to do it?"

"No."

"You're going to do it, right?"

"No."

"Are you going to do it in freestyle or best trick?"

"Neither."

"You're just trying to throw us off track, right?"

"No."

Then the commercials started.

"Tune in to X Games XI to see Travis Pastrana attempt the amazing double backflip!" What?! I was in their magazine ads, on their TV commercials, on their billboards. ESPN built up the double so that no matter what I did, I was going to disappoint everyone. All anyone watching at home would think was, "Why'd he back out? Why would he say he was going to do a double, then not even try?"

In the Best Trick contest on Thursday, the first day of X Games competition, I unveiled my cool new barspin bike. Before my first run, I hopped in a frontloader and carved out a special takeoff that would give me enough hangtime for the trick. I planned to try out the new bike in my first run of finals. When my name was called, I took off, hit the dirt takeoff—and my bike separated into two pieces. I actually was able to do the entire trick, but when I landed, I went flying off the bike and landed in the dirt with the handlebars still in my hands. The rest of the bike landed about five feet away. For my second run, I used the bike I brought for freestyle. I tried convincing the X Games to let me do a backflip with skateboarder Ryan Sheckler on my handlebars, but officials said no.

Instead, for my second run, I did a combo backflip to no-hander landing over the 75-foot jump. It was a solid trick but good for only second place. The gold medal went to Jeremy Stenberg, who landed a backflip combo over the 90-foot gap, setting a record for the longest flip in X Games history, even though 10 of us flipped the 90 footer in practice. Records, in our sport, are arbitrary.

Freestyle was next, two days later on Saturday night, and talk of the double intensified. Right before my first run of the finals, an ESPN commentator asked me for an interview. I'd already told this reporter I had no plans to try the double, so I thought this was my chance to clear the air. Instead, on live TV, she said, "So, Travis. I hear we're going to see a double backflip tonight." What? I couldn't believe it. "No. Absolutely not," I answered. "One-hundred percent no. I haven't practiced it. Haven't thought about it in a year. No double. Sorry, guys." But for three days, the double was all the ESPN broadcasters had talked about. They called it my million-dollar trick, even though I said all along that I wasn't doing it. I didn't understand why no one was listening to me. I looked bad, and I knew my run was about to be judged on what I didn't do.

That night, I put in the best run of my life. I landed a saran-wrap backflip and was the only rider who used The Wall, a quarterpipe-like obstacle. I had so much fun, and it was obvious to everyone, including the judges. I won without the double or the 360. Still, the 2005 X Games became known as The Year Travis Pastrana Didn't Do a Double Backflip. After the event, every kid who wanted my autograph also asked, "Travis, why didn't you do the double?"

About a week after the X Games, I drove up to Spokane with some friends to film for the video *Lock-n-Load.* I was excited to get out of L.A. and far away from questions about the double backflip. As soon as we got to Spokane, we built a park full of jumps. I had brought a couple of bikes with me, including the barspin bike, which we repaired after the X Games. My friend and Ogio team manager, Andy Bell, thought the barspin backflip looked easy, until he tried the trick over and over, and crashed every time. We had even modified the ramp setup for him, building an enormous step-up jump. The landing, made out of soft sand, was higher than the takeoff, which meant Andy wouldn't fall as far. This jump was different from most freestyle jumps. We pushed the metal takeoff ramp tight against the huge pile of sand so you went almost straight up and straight back down, instead of crossing a gap from takeoff to landing. Andy almost landed the barspin once, but mainly he just crashed a lot. But most important, he got up every time he crashed, which meant the consequences of falling on this jump were not high. Hmm. My inner-wheels started spinning.

If I added sand to the landing, making it even softer, moved the ramp back and hit it with more speed, I had the perfect setting for a double backflip. I had to laugh at the irony. I had come to Washington to escape the double, and now I found myself in the ideal situation to give it a try. "Dude, I bet could do a double on this jump," I said. Everyone's ears perked up. No backing out now.

This was the last day of filming and I had about 20 minutes before I had to leave for the airport. I tried the flip about 10 times, but kept bailing. I'd been giving the other riders so much hell all week that all of them let me have it.

"Commit, Travis!"

"Why are you bailing!?"

"Stop being such a wuss!"

Even the girls were heckling me. "Stop being a baby, Travis!" yelled my friend Sarah Whitmore, one of the top female motocross racers.

On the next try, I didn't make it around on the second flip, but I committed. I pulled as hard as I could and stayed on the bike. I got about three-quarters of the way around on the second flip, crashed into the sand and got pounded by the motorcycle. I tried the trick a couple more times until my body was so torn up that I had to call it a day. Blood was dripping down my arms, legs, and face. My left knee had a huge, inch-deep gouge in it. I thought my thumb and my ankle were broken, and I could barely walk. By the time I got on the plane to fly to a contest in Ibiza, in the south of Spain, I was bloody from head to toe.

I didn't think about the double for the next two weeks. But while I was in Spain, my knee got infected. When I returned home to Maryland, I took a week to recuperate from my injuries. During that time, I started thinking about the double again. I called my friend Gregg Godfrey, who was producing *Lock-n-Load,* in California.

"Don't move it," I said.

"Don't move what?"

"The ramp in Washington. Don't move it. I need to land the double flip."

A few days later, I was back in Spokane. I'd been visualizing the double for the past five days. I knew how much height I needed, knew how much time in the air I needed, and knew how hard I had to pull to get myself around two times. I also knew it was now or never.

On my way to Spokane, I invited BMX rider Reuel Erickson to drive up from Nevada for the jump. Nine years earlier, when he was 17, Reuel landed the first double backflip on a BMX bike, so I wanted his guidance. He was pumped that I'd invited him and agreed to meet me in Spokane. He told me he couldn't sleep the night before he tried the double for the first time. He also said the most important thing I could do was focus. This trick was all about confidence.

The morning of the jump, the conditions were perfect. It was October, so the air was chilly, but the sun was shining and there was barely a cloud in the sky. Andy and I got in the frontloader and added another 1,000 pounds of dirt to the backside of the landing. It was the biggest, softest, fluffiest landing I could build. But I was afraid; the jump was huge. The takeoff looked so scary, like you were staring at the side of a mountain that shot straight up. From the bottom of the ramp, you couldn't see the landing above. Still, I weighed the consequences and I knew the worst-case scenario was a broken bone. Or several. But the reward would be worth the risk.

So I put on my helmet and rode to the takeoff area. Didn't even warm up. "Get this on film," I said to Godfrey. "I'm going to land a double flip on the first try." I saw the red light on his camera turn on, and I took off.

I hit the ramp and pulled as hard as I could. I stayed on the bike, spotted the landing, then stuck my front tire into the sand and face planted into the landing area. "Holy crap! That almost worked!" I yelled. I got back on the bike and tried again. Same result. I tried a third time. Same result.

"There's too much sand," Andy said. "You would have ridden out of every one of those if the landing were hard-packed." I knew he was right, so I hopped in the bulldozer and packed the sand down. Now the conditions were perfect, but the consequences of crashing on hard-packed ground were higher. Crash this time and my body would suffer the impact of a three-story fall. "Do everything the same," I thought. "Commit. This trick is all about confidence."

On the next try, I hit the ramp, pulled as hard as I could, spotted the landing, and then felt my front—and back—tires touch down. I did it! I had landed the first double backflip on a motorcycle. I had just pulled off

"YESTERDAY'S LIMITS
WERE GONE. I'D
SET NEW ONES.
I COULD MOVE ON."

TWO,
TAKE TWO

**Everything is impossible
until someone does it.**

IT SUCKS TO BE ME

In the first part of 2006, rally racing was taking a lot of my time. My schedule was nuts. When the first Dew Tour stop rolled around, I drove through the night just to make it to Louisville on time. I got to the hotel at three in the morning, tired as hell, and went straight to my room. The hotel was filled with athletes running through the halls, screaming, partying. I put a pillow over my head and went to sleep.

When the 2006 freestyle season started, my focus had shifted to rally racing. It was my second season driving rally cars and I was determined to win the title. Unfortunately, that meant freestyle was getting even less of my attention. I went to the first stop of the Dew Tour, in Louisville, Kentucky, without any new tricks, and I lost to Nate. He's still the only guy who's ever beaten me in freestyle competition and this was the third time he did it. On the podium, I gave credit to Nate and accepted second place. No excuses.

A couple of weeks later, I was watching the TV broadcast of the contest and the commentator asked Nate about beating me. "It wasn't a big deal," he said. "I'm just better than Travis." Excuse me? I was stunned. I grabbed my phone and called Andy Bell, team manager at Ogio, which sponsors Nate and me. "Tell Nate to get off the couch, get on his bike, and start working his butt off. I'm coming with tricks he hasn't even imagined."

Then I sent Nate a text: "Game on. Get ready for the next round."

I was so fired up that I hit the foam pit the next day. By the second Dew Tour stop, in Denver, I'd invented the Super flip and the Super Indian flip. I also had the double backflip dialed into the foam and planned to throw it in my freestyle run in Denver. I called every rider and told them what tricks I was working on and how I was doing them. If Nate was going to win, I wanted him to win with every rider throwing Superman flips and doubles. In my mind, he wasn't going to win another contest all year. He certainly wasn't going to beat me. But a few days before the contest, my agent called. "I know you have the double," he said, sounding less than confident. "But this isn't the right time. Save it for the X Games." For once, I listened.

In the 10 years I've been involved in freestyle, I've obviously had a lot of fun. That's why I ride freestyle. The competitions are a blast and I look forward to them all year. But I had done just about everything I could in freestyle and was about to walk away when Nate pulled me back in. I didn't really care that Nate thought he was better than me. And yet, I did care. He pissed me off. He motivated me. And he fueled the greatest, and most fun, year of my life.

Throughout that summer, I worked on the double with more determination and focus than I'd worked on any trick. Even though I'd landed the double in Spokane, the questions didn't stop. In fact, the pressure was even more intense. Some people said they thought those photos in *ESPN The Magazine* were fake! Those who did believe I'd landed the double said the setup was too easy. If I wanted to prove the trick was possible, I had to land it in a contest—no special step-up jump, no sand landing. After a lot of trial and error, I figured out the timing, the feel, and the ramp dimensions. A couple of weeks before the X Games, I called ESPN and told them I needed a special freestyle ramp. Usually they'll make changes for a rider if they think the reason is worthwhile. In other words, if it will result in good TV. But I was told, "We'll think about it." They didn't believe me. I was the Boy Who Cried Double Backflip.

I had enough experience to know that I couldn't land the double off a standard jump. When I didn't hear back in a week, my dad called again. "Look," he said, when he finally got someone on the phone. "My son is going to try a double flip. To be successful, he needs a special ramp. But he's going to do it either way. Do you want to see my son die on national television?" That got their attention. They agreed to help.

If I had my way, I would have thrown the double in my freestyle run. But ESPN wasn't willing to alter the ramps on the freestyle course, because it would inconvenience the other riders. So I agreed to attempt it in the best trick contest, where a special ramp and landing would be set up just for me. Unfortunately, best trick was scheduled for Friday night. That meant if I got hurt, I wouldn't be able to compete in the three events that followed on Saturday and Sunday: freestyle, supermoto, and rally racing, the newest X Games event and the one I was most excited about. If I crashed, got hurt, and knocked myself out of those events, I would lose the opportunity to make $200,000, since each win was worth 50 grand.

All day Friday, I was a wreck. Do it. Don't do it. I couldn't make up my mind, and every person I asked had a different answer. Most of my friends thought I shouldn't do it. "We know you can do it, Travis," Kenny said. "So you don't have to do it. It's not worth it. You don't have to prove anything."

I arrived at best trick practice late because I had practice for my other three events. I also had to stop by the medical tent and have my knee drained—I had a torn MCL and meniscus damage in my right knee. When I got to the STAPLES Center, where the event was taking place, my ramp wasn't set up. I needed to take a few practice runs to see if it felt right, so I asked one of the course designers about prepping the jump. "Sure. We spend time moving the ramp back, changing the angles, and then you won't even do it. I've heard it before. You just want drama. You want people to think you're going to do a double backflip." For two years, I'd listened to the doubters and disbelievers and I couldn't take it any longer. "Move it back," I said.

IT'S GOOD TO BE ME

Around 4:30, I woke up to someone knocking on my door. I was annoyed. I got up, opened the door, and there was 16-year-old Ryan Sheckler flanked by two drop-dead gorgeous, twentysomething blonde girls. "Hey, Trav," he said. "These girls are staying with me, but I have an early day tomorrow and my mom's going to wake me up around six. I'd prefer not to have them in my bed when she gets there. Is it cool if they stay with you?"

Man," I thought. "What a friend."

"WHEN I REALIZED THE DOUBLE MIGHT ACTUALLY BE POSSIBLE, I TIGHTENED MY GRIP ON THE HANDLEBARS."

DRESSED TO THRILL

When I started seriously considering doing the double backflip at X, I called my clothing sponsor, Thor, and told them I wanted a special outfit. I knew that if I landed that trick, photos of my jump would be the most viewed photos in motocross history. "Everyone tries to look so cool for the X Games," I said. "I want the most ridiculous outfit you can dream up." I wanted people to curse my name when they had to run photos of the double backflip. I expected to show up in Los Angeles and be handed a pink tutu, but instead, their designers dreamed up a lumberjack outfit with a "been there, crashed that" logo on the front and a giant "thumbs-up" on the butt. Of course, my plan backfired. Everyone said the getup was "so cool."

As soon as the ramp was raised, rumors started flying. People had heard I was thinking about the double, but now everyone in the crowd knew it was true. I still wasn't 100% sure I could pull it off. But knowing that everyone expected a double, and that almost as many people doubted I would try it, gave me the extra push I needed.

I took one practice jump on the new ramp and it felt right. As the other riders took their first runs, the ramp sat unused on the course, but it was the focus of all conversation. Will he? Won't he? I dropped in for my first run and hit the shorter ramp. I did a Super flip that I thought would put me in the lead. But it didn't. The competition was so stiff that a trick that would have won the contest a month earlier now put me in fourth place. Only the double would win. As I rode back to the start area, past the rows of fans, a little boy, maybe five years old, put his arm out to stop me. I thought he wanted a high-five, but instead he grabbed my arm. "Don't do it, Travis!" he said, tears in his eyes. "My Mommy says when you die—you're dead forever." Ah … kids.

About midway through the second runs, a course official approached me. "What's the verdict?" he asked. "Are you or aren't you?" One of the other riders had used my super kicker, but now if I was going to do the double, they needed to raise the front and push the takeoff back 10 feet. If not, they weren't going to bother.

The other riders weren't big confidence boosters. Ronnie Faisst echoed Kenny's sentiments. He told me he knew I could do it, so I didn't have to. And he was praying for me. "Besides," he said, "I don't want to scrape you off the concrete." Nate kneeled at the bottom of the landing and prayed for me. Brian Deegan wished me good luck, but looked amused. I needed backup.

First, I called my dad in Maryland to tell him I was going to do a double flip. I found out later that he had called my team manager, Ron, and told him to take the spark plug out of my bike and run. "Don't ask questions," he said. "Just do it!"

"This is stupid," he said. "Don't do it. You're going to crash."

"Dad, I love you. But I have to do it. I have to try. I'm confident. I know I will make it."

"All right, then. I'm going to the bar."

I couldn't ask my mom. She'd flown in the night before and hadn't stopped crying since she landed. A bunch of my friends had gathered at the top of the roll-in, so I went to them. I turned to one of them, Hubert, with the perfect solution. "Rock, paper, scissors," I said. "One game.

BEFORE MY RUN,
I VISUALIZED
THE DOUBLE
BACKFLIP OVER
AND OVER.
UNTIL NOW, I
DIDN'T REALIZE
HOW FUNNY
THAT LOOKED TO
EVERYONE ELSE.

MY FRIENDS SWARMED ME WHEN I LANDED THE DOUBLE. THE BEST PART ABOUT THIS PHOTO? I DON'T KNOW THE GUY IN THE WHITE TANK TOP. HE WAS JUST A KID WHO GOT TO ME FIRST. AND THE FIRST PERSON I CELEBRATED WITH.

Winner decides." I rule this game. The other guy always throws rock. So I threw paper. Hubert threw scissors.

"You're doing a double backflip," Hubert said.

"Raise the ramp," I said to the official.

With two riders to go, the course builders started placing 2x4s under the base of the ramp. When they finished, the ramp looked so unstable that I thought it was going to crumble when I took off. Just then, my close friend and team manager, Ron Meredith, walked up to me. "Travis," he said, "I know you can do this. You're not going to do something you don't think you can do. If you say you can do this, I believe you. And damn it, do not second guess yourself." He was right. I could do this. I was still pretty sure I was going to crash. But I was okay with that. I was ready. I was focused. Then I heard another voice from a few feet behind me.

"Don't do it, Travis! Think about the money. If you get hurt, you're throwing away your X Games." It was my agent. No time to be logical now. I had a double backflip to do.

I rode to the top of the roll-in and was stopped by a guy wearing a headset. The event was being broadcast live and I had to wait for a commercial break. I took a deep breath and looked out over the arena. It was the first time I stopped to take in my surroundings. The entire crowd was on its feet. I couldn't believe the energy. I looked to my right, where the halfpipe was set up for the BMX contest that would take place later that night, and I saw BMX riders Kevin Robinson and Chad Kagy at the top of the ramp. They were huddled together and looked concerned. "Wow," I thought. "This is intense." I realized then that no matter what happened, whether I crashed or rode away, I was going to live in that moment. It was the most incredible feeling and I didn't want it to end. Then the red light on the camera turned on and we were back from commercial.

"It's your time," the official said. "Go."

I closed my eyes, took another deep breath, then rolled down the ramp. Over the next few seconds, my

WHAT A BREAK

When something goes wrong on a jump, time slows down. While I'm flying through the air, I am processing a lot of information. Most important, I'm deciding what part of my body I'm going to sacrifice. I decide that by asking myself a few questions: How much time do I have to recover? What part of my body is the healthiest right now? What must I avoid injuring? Then, these three scenarios run through my mind:

OPTION 1: Land forward on the bike and take the impact through my upper body.

WHY: I already have an ankle, knee, or back injury. Maximum recovery time for an upper-body injury is short, about three months.

WORST-CASE: My upper body isn't as strong, so I'm going to break my wrists, arms, shoulders, or a few ribs.

OPTION 2: Lean back on the motorcycle and take the impact through my torso and lower body.

WHY: My upper body is already injured or weak. The chance of a concussion is lessened.

WORST-CASE: If I hit hard enough, a broken back. But it's stronger than my body. Recovery time could be as short as three weeks (cracked vertebrae) to forever (paralysis).

OPTION 3: Bail in mid-air.

WHY: To get away from the bike and prevent it from impaling me on a bad fall.

WORST-CASE: Blown knees. This is a tough decision for every rider. If you have bad knees or ankles, they will get much worse. If they're healthy, it's a good option. But they'll never be the same again. Recovery time could be as much as a year for a full knee reconstruction, and possibly career- (but not life-) threatening.

IT SUCKS TO BE ME

In October 2006, I went to Madrid for a freestyle contest called X-Fighters. I'd barely slept in the two months since landing the double backflip at the X Games. It was a circus everywhere I went. I took a redeye to Spain and arrived the morning of the event. I had so many interviews, photo shoots, and signings that I barely had time to practice. I was living off Red Bull and donuts.

I won the event, which was fun. But when I tried to leave the arena to go to the afterparty with the other riders, I was stopped. The other guys walked right through. I signed autographs and gave interviews for two hours. Back at the hotel, the same thing happened. More cameras, more microphones, more autographs. I love my fans, but it was two in the morning. I was hungry, tired, sore, and bitter.

I finally broke away and got to the party around four, the last guy to arrive. All my friends were having a great time and there were beautiful girls everywhere. But as soon as I walked in, every dude in the bar surrounded me for an autograph. After signing, I finally made my way to the bar, had a few drinks, and took off.

THE DOUBLE WAS THE FIRST TRICK THAT EVERYONE IN THE ARENA UNDERSTOOD. THEY KNEW HOW DIFFICULT AND DANGEROUS IT WAS—AND I WANTED TO CELEBRATE WITH THEM ALL (OPPOSITE).

mind was flooded with thoughts. I thought about crashing. I thought about how I would handle the crash, what I would do, how I would fall. I was sure I would crash. But I didn't want to die.

As my tires hit the bottom of the ramp, everything felt right. "It's just like the foam pit at home," I thought. "I've done this 1,000 times." I rode up the ramp, launched the bike, and initiated the first flip. The next two seconds felt like an eternity. I remember each second as if it lasted 10.

On the first rotation, I didn't pull as hard as I could have, because I thought I had too much height and was going to overshoot the landing. But when I came around and spotted the landing, I realized I was spinning too slow. I was going to land short. What I didn't realize until I saw the video was that I hadn't factored in everything. Directly above the jump, in the exact location where I reached the peak of my first flip, hung a giant floodlight. My head missed smashing into it by only a few feet. Had I hit it, I would have been knocked off course and crashed from nearly 50 feet above the floor of the Staples Center.

I needed to speed up my second rotation. But in the more than 1,000 attempts I'd thrown into my foam pit, I was never able to do that. Until that night. I pulled so hard that the second flip sped up perfectly. I couldn't believe it. After the first flip, I was so convinced I was going to crash that when I came around the second time and spotted the landing—dirt!—I almost crashed out of shock. When I realized landing this trick might actually be possible, I tightened my grip on the handlebars.

And then…

I landed. Like a ton of bricks. I collapsed onto the bike, but kept my balance. I rolled to a stop and jumped off my bike. I threw my hands in the air and started running around like a maniac. I didn't know where I was going or who I was looking for. It was such a surreal moment. Euphoric. I was thinking, "Did that really happen? Is this happening? No … freakin' … way!"

I ran down the ramp and then up the side of the dirt landing and was tackled by a group of friends. When I watched the video, I realized the first person to reach me, the first guy I hugged, was actually a random drunk guy in a white tank top who'd wandered out onto the course. I was so out of my mind, I thought he was a friend, so I hugged him and snapped a photo on his disposable camera. Then security grabbed him and took him away.

The next few minutes were chaos, all hugs, tears, camera flashes and screaming. I dove off the dirt pile and log rolled down the side. I

IT'S GOOD TO BE ME

As I was leaving the bar, I noticed a beautiful Spanish girl standing outside. She was trying to get into the party but didn't have a pass. She recognized me, smiled, and pointed at my pass. I shook my head no. "Sorry. I can't help you." I started to flag down a cab, but she stopped me and pointed to her car. She didn't speak English. "A ride?" I asked. "Cool. My hotel?" She nodded. I figured she knew the word "hotel."

Instead, she drove me to this great house. Her house. She parked in the driveway and took me inside. As we were walking up to her room, I thought, "Man, I love my life. This makes up for the rest of my night!"

The next morning, we walked downstairs. "Aeropuerto?" I asked. She nodded. I followed her into the kitchen where two guys were having breakfast.

"Hello! Wow! Travis Pastrana! No way!"

No way is right. This wasn't her house. It was her parents' house. Her dad and brother were making eggs, and they spoke perfect English. Apparently, they were big fans. I spent the morning talking about freestyle in the States. Talk about awkward. But I finally had a great meal. Then the girl and her brother drove me to my hotel and bid me *adios*.

WHEN I LANDED THE DOUBLE, MY MOM WAS THE FIRST PERSON I THOUGHT OF. WHEN I FINALLY FOUND HER, I GAVE HER A HUGE HUG. "THANK YOU FOR SUPPORTING ME," I SAID.

MOM SPEAKS

The truth? I didn't see it. For most of the contest, I stood in the stands on the first level. A girl from ESPN told me she would take me down to the course when I was ready. I thought we would walk down and hop over the barricade, so I waited until a few minutes before his run. "Take me down, I'm ready." She took me to some steps. Then through a hallway. Then we got in an elevator. As the doors opened, I heard everyone yelling and screaming. I ran out to the landing and Travis was running to the top of the hill, celebrating. I'd missed it. I wanted to find that girl again and tell her it was all right. I knew it was a good thing I didn't see Travis jump. It was God's way of protecting me. I don't think my heart could have taken it. I ran and met him at the top of the hill and hugged him. He said when he landed, his first thought was, "Wow!" His second was, "I hope my mom is okay."

saw my mom running toward me. When she finally reached me, I gave her a huge hug and thanked her for being there, for supporting me. I know it's tough to sit on the sidelines and watch. I tried to experience that moment the way I did the jump itself. I wanted to slow time down and enjoy every second. I knew I would never experience anything like that again. I've had a lot of amazing moments, but nothing compares to that night. The double backflip was the first trick that everyone in the arena, from the riders to the fans, understood. They felt what I was feeling. They knew the level of commitment it took to drop into that ramp that night, and they understood the improbably of me riding away.

I left the arena on such a high. Most people expected me to party the night away. Instead, I went to the medical room, had my knee drained, grabbed a milkshake and burger at Jack in the Box, then went to my room and fell asleep. I had three more events that weekend and practice started at eight the next morning.

When I woke up the next day, I turned on my cell phone to find it flooded with calls from friends and family. My favorite was from a group of six of my friends from Maryland. They were going on a trip together and were on a flight during the broadcast. The airline they were flying had DIRECTV, so they were able to watch the contest. Word spread throughout the plane that I was a friend of theirs, so when I landed the double, the entire plane erupted with cheers. My friends jumped out of their seats and were running through the aisle screaming. The flight attendant from first class came running to the back of the plane in horror when she heard the screams. When they told her what happened, she started screaming, too.

Those calls, I appreciate. But there was another side to that accomplishment. I thought that by landing the double, I would prove that the trick was possible and that I could move on. But now people expect me to throw double backflips at every contest.

"When will you do it again, Travis?"

"Do you want to come to our demo and throw the double next weekend?"

"You did it once. It can't be that hard."

"When are you doing a triple?"

The other riders are feeling it, too. Now, fans expect everyone to throw double backflips.

Even after 10 years in freestyle and racing motocross, I have

DAD SPEAKS

I was at a restaurant with some friends. It closed at 10, but the owner's a friend, so he kept the bar open so we could watch the X Games. I was a lot quieter than usual. A few minutes before his second run, Travis called. He said, "I'm going to do it." I said, "I know you can. I wish you wouldn't. But I know you can." He said he'd call me from the hospital. Then I said, "I love you," and he said "I love you," and we hung up. I knew he didn't have a lot of time. It was a quick check-in call to say "hi" while he was still healthy. He called because he needed to hear, from me, that it was possible. I think I said that the best I could without totally believing it. I immediately got the same feeling in my chest and throat that I get when he's lined up at a starting gate—I call it my "Dad" feeling. When he landed that trick, it hit so perfectly. There was a lot of amazement and relief and hollering and screaming. Unbelievable. It was a night I never want to go through again—and a night I wouldn't have wanted to miss.

been able to remain fairly anonymous outside the action sports world. Not anymore. I can't believe how often I am recognized. I used to hop on planes unnoticed. I loved that. I didn't want to be any more famous than I already was. And like I've said, I don't like to fly. I get nauseous as soon as I sit down. I never tell anyone my real name because that would lead to a long conversation about Me. Not my favorite topic. Instead, when people ask what I do, I like to have fun. I say I hang drywall or pack parachutes for a living.

But since the double backflip, I haven't been on many flights where the person next to me hasn't recognized me. I don't know how movie stars do it. The hardest part is that, to most people, I'm not Travis Pastrana anymore. I'm "Hey! There's that Double Backflip Guy!" I liked being anonymous. I can't go to a race and watch my friends ride or sit in the stands at a skateboard contest. That's the part of celebrity that's tough.

The week after the X Games, I was inundated with calls offering me $200,000 for two days of racing and jumping in Europe. I got offers to go to Australia and make nearly $100,000 in a weekend. But I said no to all of them. It's not that I couldn't use the money. But I'm content with the life I live. I like spending my off days riding with friends. And now that I'm racing rally cars, I have very few off days. Not many people have the opportunity to make that kind of money, but that money would cost me too much. Sometimes I wonder if the double backflip already has.

NOTHING I
COULD SAY
COULD TOP THE
THOUSAND
WORDS THIS
PHOTO'S
ALREADY
WORTH.

THE
Always trust your co-driver.
BIG JUMP

Until recently, motorcycles have been my life. And while it's probably strange to see me behind the wheel of a one-ton vehicle with a steering wheel and a roll cage, it actually makes a lot of sense. It's time to do something different. I've accomplished about all that I can on two wheels. Why not try four? After all, I've been driving four-wheelers as long as I've been riding motorcycles. My first vehicle was a go-kart my parents gave me when I was two. Soon I was driving (and racing and crashing and back flipping) anything I could—go-karts, lawn mowers, tractors, jeeps. I started driving my dad's pickup truck when I was too small to see over the steering wheel. I have always loved to drive fast.

As a teenager, I became a huge fan of **rally car racing**. I watched international rally races on TV and imagined I was one of the drivers. When I was 17, I found out that one of my gear sponsors, Alpinestars, also sponsored the Subaru World Rally Team. I couldn't believe it. I called my team manager and told him I wanted in. "We'll see what we can do," he said.

A short time later, Alpinestars owner Gabriele Mazzarolo invited me to Great Britain for the final race of the 2001 World Rally Championship season and to test-drive a Subaru World Rally car. The day after the race, I took a three-day instructional class with Mark Lovell, a British rally champion who had moved to the States to race in the U.S. Rally Championship. He flew back to Europe just to train me. I'd only had my driver's license a year, and I was being taught to drive a $750,000 race-car by one of the best drivers in the world. What an experience. I loved the feeling of flying around hairpin turns and over jumps at 120mph. It wasn't like other forms of car racing, where you take the same line every lap. It was so much like Supercross that, by the time I left, I was hooked.

I knew that whenever I accomplished all that I set out to do in motocross, I was going to do all I could to get into rally racing. From then on, every time I got hurt and had to stop riding motorcycles, I practiced driving. If I was near a track, I raced go-karts. My team manager at Alpinestars got me a custom #199 Renspeed shifter kart that I topped out at more than 100mph. It goes from 0 to 100 and back to 0 in under 10 seconds. That's faster than a Ferrari. Trust me. I've tested it. When I was 19, I entered the Shifter Kart SuperNationals in Las Vegas and finished 28th in the nation.

Rally Car Racing (Ra•lly•car•ra•cing)

NOUN: A form of car racing featuring a driver and co-driver in street legal cars on "stages" or closed sections of roads. One car runs the course at a time, in time-trial fashion. The co-driver navigates and communicates upcoming conditions to the driver, who speeds around and over natural obstacles such as blind crests, jumps, turns, and dips.

That year, I also raced in the Porsche Michelin Supercup at Indianapolis Motor Speedway and entered a local demolition derby in Maryland.

Then in 2004, Rally America started a new championship series, but money was still scarce. Without sponsors, drivers were forced to pay their way to races and to maintain their cars. American rally racing isn't as big-time as World Rally, where drivers have factory sponsorships and drive million-dollar cars. My parents and my agent didn't understand why, of all the motor-sports available to me, I picked rally. "Why don't you go into NASCAR, where you can make a lot money?" they asked. "There are teams that would love to have you." Once again, people thought I was wasting my talent.

But who needs a lot of money? I'd be happy if I could simply make a living racing and still have fun. I like the creativity of rally racing. I like the freedom. I like the feeling of flying through trees and between hills and over jumps. It's the perfect mix of Supercross, freestyle motocross, and car racing. Sure, there is a possibility I could make millions of dollars in NASCAR, but I would get bored. I knew that becoming good enough to make a living in rally would be a long road, but it would be a fun drive. My agent finally gave in and gave me his (semi) full support.

In 2004, Subaru and Vermont SportsCar entered me in three races to see if I could compete against experienced drivers. This was before I had even signed a sponsorship contract with them. My first race was the Sno*Drift Rally in Atlanta, Michigan. It did not go well. I spent most of the race digging out of snow banks. The other drivers

EVEN BEFORE MY FEET COULD REACH THE PEDALS, I WAS DRIVING ANYTHING LEFT UNATTENDED FOR TOO LONG. TODAY, IF IT HAS WHEELS, I WANT TO DRIVE IT, TEST ITS LIMITS, AND PUSH IT FURTHER THAN MOST PEOPLE THINK IT CAN GO.

IT SUCKS TO BE ME

In 2006, I was selected to represent the United States in The Race of Champions in Paris, France. The Race of Champions is an international race featuring national teams made up of an off-road (Dakar Rally, Baja 1000) driver and a circuit (NASCAR, F1) driver. In 2005, I partnered with Jeff Gordon in the race, but I lost in the first round. This time, I was excited to be paired up with my friend and NEXTEL Cup champ, Jimmie Johnson. He would drive the pavement legs of the race and I would drive the rally sections. A week before we were to leave for Paris, I got a text message from Jimmie: "Broke my wrist. I'm out." He was at a charity golf tournament and fell off the roof of a golf cart. Sounded like something I would do. A few days later, Formula One driver Scott Speed was named as his replacement. I flew to Paris, psyched to team up with Scott. But two days before the race, Scott hurt his wrist in a testing accident in Jerez, Spain! He was out. It was the day before the race and too late to fly another driver to Paris. It looked like Team USA would have to forfeit.

WITH MY BRAINIER HALF—MY CO-DRIVER, CHRISTIAN EDSTROM.

figured I would spend my career digging myself out. But my second race, the Rim of the World Rally in Palmdale, California, changed the way the other drivers looked at me. And it changed the way I looked at my co-driver, Christian Edstrom.

Vermont SportsCar paired me with Christian shortly before the Sno*Drift. He's Swedish, seven years older than me, and wore goofy-looking wire rimmed glasses. (In late 2006, Christian got laser surgery, so I can't bust on his goofy glasses any more.) I spent five minutes with him and thought, "This guy is the biggest nerd I've ever met!" And those are big words coming from me. But he was supposed to be the best co-driver in the U.S. He'd been racing since 1997 and had worked with some of the best drivers in the U.S. and Canada. He knows the Rally America rulebook inside and out. He should: He wrote it. I didn't think the co-driver was that important and wanted to give the job to a friend, but my sponsors insisted I race with Christian. I learned the wisdom of their decision at the 2004 Rim of the World Rally, the second of the three 2004 races.

Rim of the World was my first rally on gravel roads, and it's run on one of the hairiest courses in the country. One stage, called Del Sur, winds through the Angeles National Forest. Huge rocks, ledges, and trees are

IT'S GREAT TO BE ME

I have to admit, when something bad happens in my life, I usually smile, knowing that something better is on its way. After Scott got hurt, I got an idea. At first, I presented it to the race organizers as a joke: What if I race every leg of the event? They didn't laugh. It was unprecedented to allow one driver to represent an entire nation. But they decided to let the other drivers decide. Those guys wouldn't have approved any other solo driver, but I was on an underdog American team, and the Americans are supposed to get killed. They thought they'd kick my ass in the first round, so they said yes. The organizers changed the race format to give me time to switch from car to car. I called my dad and told him he wouldn't believe who my new teammate was: Me!

"Team USA is going to suck," I told him. "But we are going to have the most fun." Jimmie came out to the race to cheer me on. In the end, I won the first round, and the second, and beat 1995 World Rally champion Colin McCrae and Formula One star David Coulthard in the semi-final. After the race, reality hit. I'd just beaten Coulthard, one of the 10 best drivers on the planet. What the hell are the chances of that? Well, with my luck, I guess they're pretty good. And I'd rather be lucky than good any day.

scattered all over the course, and it is lined with more cliffs than any other stage in the series. The course makes Pikes Peak look like CandyLand.

Before that stage, Christian walked up to me and said, "We can win this stage." I thought he had lost his mind. "We have an advantage. Everyone else is going to be scared, but this is what you live for. I know what you've accomplished, and I think you're a bit crazy. We're going to use that to our advantage." He didn't know me from Adam, but he had complete confidence in me. I realized I needed to have that same level of confidence in him.

Unlike NASCAR or Indy racing, where you drive in a circle and take the same line again and again, every stage of every rally course is different, and the courses change year to year. Races last two to three days and are made up of 15 to 25 stages, or timed sprints, of distances between five and 30 miles. Before the race, co-drivers are handed computer-generated notes on each stage. Drivers aren't told anything about the course until they are actually racing. The co-drivers act as our eyes. They tell us when to turn, speed up, slow down, and when there is an obstacle on the course or a gap to jump. At 120 miles an hour, I don't have time to question Christian's instructions. Even when I want to.

HOW DO I STAY SO CALM WHILE DRIVING 100MPH? THE ANSWER IS THE GUY RIDING SHOTGUN.

AH, THE
ROUGH LIFE
OF A RACE-
CAR DRIVER.

About halfway through the Del Sur stage, we flew around a tight corner and hit a long straightaway. Christian called out details on the next section from his notes: "Flat jump over crest 350," he said. In plain English, that meant, "Keep it pinned. You're about to fly the length of three football fields over a steep, blind cliff, Dukes of Hazzard style."

I glanced at Christian and thought, "Can I trust this crazy guy sitting beside me? What if he's wrong?" I knew he was thinking, "Can I trust this crazy guy sitting beside me? What if he panics and kills us?" For some reason, we both decided the answer to the "trust" question was yes. So I hit the gas and sailed off the side of a cliff.

Although the car was never more than five feet above the ground, we would fall 500 feet to the rocky ground below if I veered off course or failed to make it to the other side. I held my breath as we sailed a little more than 300 yards, then exhaled as we landed as smoothly as if we'd just jumped a puddle. I kept the gas pinned, took Christian's next directions, and finished the race. He called the course perfectly and I drove my butt off. We took second place in the stage and fourth overall. We didn't win the stage as Christian predicted, but we'd done better than anyone expected. Suddenly, the drivers who had written me off were looking at

WHEN I TOLD MY SPONSOR I HAD A LITTLE EXTRA MONEY TO BURN, THEY DIDN'T THINK I MEANT IT LITERALLY. BUT AFTER SINKING $250,000 INTO A BAJA 1000 RIDE, I WATCHED MY INVESTMENT GO UP IN FLAMES. I FLIPPED IT 500 MILES INTO THE RACE AND THE TRUCK EXPLODED. BUT IT MADE FOR A WARM SPOT TO SLEEP THAT NIGHT (OPPOSITE).

me in a different light. I'd proven I could drive. I'd also learned the importance of that nerdy guy sitting in the passenger seat.

In 2005, with Christian still by my side, I raced my first season as a professional rally car driver. Although I'd proven I could drive, the other drivers still had mixed feelings about my turning pro. I came in with a factory sponsorship and top-line equipment, a level they had worked their whole lives to reach. In American rally racing, even the best guys aren't driving million-dollar cars like World Rally drivers. Almost every driver is his own mechanic, and probably built his car, ground up, from a $600 clunker he bought when he was 17 years old. They work their way up through the ranks. I started at the top.

That first season, I showed potential but I crashed too often. After 2005, few people had high expectations for my sophomore season. But I learned to look at the big picture. My driving matured and I stopped crashing. In 2006, I finished every race on the podium. I became the youngest American rally champion when I won the 2006 Rally America National Championship at age 23. Of course, I didn't do it alone. Rally, unlike motocross, is a team sport. There are two guys in the car. To win a championship, I had to learn how to be a teammate.

When I race motocross or compete in freestyle, I only have to rely on myself. Sure, it takes a team effort to prepare, but when it comes down to the race, I'm the only guy on the track. I pre-walk the courses and know every turn, bump, and landing. So it's a weird feeling to trust someone else to read the course for me. Rally is the first team sport I truly enjoy. I tell my friends that our team is really more like a relationship. Christian and I bicker like a husband and wife. Actually, I think I spend more time with Christian than his wife does. I have a hard time winning an argument, though: He was the 1997 college Quiz Bowl champion.

The best thing about being part of a team is the opportunity to share my experiences with someone. After a motocross race, I would rehash the race with my parents or friends. But they weren't out there on the bike with me so they couldn't understand what I'd experienced. But Christian and I go through the same emotions, have the same fears, and see the race from the same point of view. It's cool to be able to share those experiences.

The other cool part of rally is the longevity. I can race until I'm an old man. After the Del Sur stage, while Christian and I were sitting in the car going over notes, another driver pulled up and got out of his car. "I'll tell you, that's just like a motocross track!" he said to no one in particular.

I couldn't believe what I was seeing. The driver was Bruce Brown, the director of *The Endless Summer* and the guy who made the 1971 motocross film *On Any Sunday*. The guy's almost 70! Bruce made the movie that turned the world on to motocross—the movie that got my dad interested in racing motorcycles. And now I'm racing against him in a rally car! As they say: With age, get a cage. I realized I could compete in rally for another 50 years and have as much fun as I do racing dirt bikes.

So what's in my future? That's a tough question. The thing is, I'm not much of a planner. I take every opportunity that comes at me and make the most of it. Most people make lists, like "Things I want to do before I'm 30." I couldn't begin to make that kind of list because I couldn't dream up the things I will have the opportunity to do in the next seven years. Had I made that list 10 years ago, I guarantee landing a double back-flip, winning the Rally America Championship, blowing up a $250,000 truck in the Baja 1000, and driving NEXTEL Cup champion Jimmie Johnson's leg of the Race of Champions would not have been on it. I'm not that inventive.

But that doesn't mean I don't have goals. This year, I'm racing a full Rally America schedule, along with three World Rally Championship races—the big leagues. This is going to be my most dedicated racing season since 2003, my last full year in Supercross. In 2008, I'll race a full World Rally Championship season—the most difficult series in rally racing. The races take place in 16 countries, which means I'll be spending a lot of time overseas. Only one U.S. driver has ever won a European rally race—John Buffum, in 1983, the year I was born. My goal is not just to win a race, but to win an overall World Rally Championship. Unfortunately, I'm not good enough. Yet. But I will get there because I will put in the time and I've surrounded myself with guys I trust, like Christian.

When Subaru and I first started discussing a move to World Rally, they told me they wanted to hire a co-driver with international experience to give me a better chance at success. In World Rally, teams pre-drive the course and co-drivers take their own notes on each stage. The notes are not computer generated like in American rally racing. But the guys at Subaru didn't understand the level of dedication Christian has shown and how much he's done for me. It was like asking me to switch wives. In my opinion, Christian is the best co-driver in the world. The chance to race in the World Rally Championship is a dream. And he's coming with me.

I don't know how long it will take to achieve my goal of winning the WRC, but it doesn't matter. When I was four years old, my goal was to win

DAD

ME

GRANDMA

THE PASTRANA FAMILY GATHERS FOR THANKSGIVING, 2006. WONDER WHY I'M SO COMPETITIVE? WOULD YOU WANT TO BE THE LEAST ATHLETIC GUY IN THIS FAMILY?

an AMA Supercross championship in the 250 division. I chased that dream my whole life and never accomplished it. That's okay. What matters is that I pursued that goal, and when my time ran out, I knew I had given it everything I could.

If I win a World Rally Championship one day, I will probably lose some of my fire for the sport. I've never been one to stick with a goal any longer than I needed to accomplish it. At that point, rally racing would become what freestyle is to me now: something I love and a way to have fun. I'll likely move on to my next challenge. But I will always return to my roots. As for freestyle, I can't say I'm retiring; I'm just taking a leave of absence to chase another dream. I still have a $100,000 foam pit in my backyard that I plan to use as much as possible, and I'll drop in at an occasional contest. I'm not done with motocross, either. I've just run out of time to try to be the best. At some point, you have to decide what you're willing to sacrifice to be the best. And right now, I'm willing to sacrifice freestyle because I feel I've accomplished my goals. But that's not to say I won't come back. I'm still young.

No matter what my future has in store, I'm grateful to have had the best 23 years imaginable. Most of my friends my age are just getting out of college and dreaming of the future. They have so many goals. They are starting their first jobs and dreaming of being rich and famous. They want to buy their dream house in a fancy city and own their dream car. They're at a point in their lives where they're just finding out who they are.

I'm only 23, but I already know exactly who I am. And I know that houses and money and cars and fame are not the things that make me happy. I've experienced all of that. I bought the house of my dreams at 18. But the house of my dreams is five miles from the home I grew up in, and five minutes from Grandma. I had the car of my dreams at 18, a Corvette, and I flipped it and almost killed a good friend. Now I drive a pickup. I've traveled and seen the world, and now all I want to do is spend time at home. I would be happy sitting on a farm with friends, a few bikes, a go-kart, and farm equipment. I've learned that if you chase money, you'll spend very little time doing what you love. But if you chase what you love, the money will come. I am happy because I do what I love every day and I'm proud of everything I've accomplished. And I've had a hell of a lot of fun along the way.

WAIT! ONE MORE THING. REMEMBER THAT JUMP I SAID I WANTED TO DO? GRAND CANYON ... GIRL IN A BIKINI ...

FRONT COVER: Simon Cudby
BACK COVER (from top to bottom): Pastrana family collection; Allen Kee/WireImage.com; Markus Paulsen; Jared Souney
SPINE: Simon Cudby

TITLE PAGE
pp. 2-3: Markus Paulsen

FOREWORD
p. 8: Lars Gange/rally.subaru.com

INTRODUCTION
p. 12: Malcolm McCassy

CHAPTER 1: LEARNING TO JUMP
p. 15: Paul Buckley; pp. 17-20, 22-24, 26: Pastrana family collection

CHAPTER 2: THE JUMP TO FREESTYLE
pp. 29, 33-39, 41: Pastrana family collection; p. 31: Alicia Alexander;
p. 42: Courtesy of Fleshwound Films

CHAPTER 3: A DOUBLES ROUTINE
pp. 45, 48-49, 54: Pastrana family collection; p. 46: Andy Bell/Ogio; p. 46: Brian Porter;
pp. 47, 52: Matt Salacuse, p. 56: Godfrey Entertainment/nitrocircus.com

CHAPTER 4: MAKING A SPLASH
pp. 59, 63, 65, 67, 69-71, 73, 75, 77-79: Ricky Ephrom; pp. 61, 66:
Allen Kee/WireImage.com; pp. 62, 68, 72: Pastrana family collection

CHAPTER 5: MY WORLDS COLLIDE
pp. 81-84, 86: Pastrana family collection; p. 85: Nicole Mancuso; p. 91: Simon Cudby

CHAPTER 6: THE GRAND PLUNGE
p. 93: Jack Guthrie/skydiveutah.com; pp. 95, 99-104: Joe Bonnello; p. 97: Malcolm McCassy

CHAPTER 7: FULL CIRCLE
pp. 109, 114-115, 119-121: Allen Kee/WireImage.com; p. 113: Godfrey
Entertainment/nitrocircus.com; p. 116: Pastrana family collection; pp. 122-123: Bo Bridges

CHAPTER 8: FIRST TO TWO
p. 127: Mike Ehrmann/WireImage.com; pp. 130, 136-137: Nate Christenson;
p. 138: Godfrey Entertainment/nitrocircus.com

CHAPTER 9: TWO, TAKE TWO
pp. 141, 155: Erik Lars Bakke; pp. 144-145, 148: Christian Pondella;
p. 147: Malcolm McCassy; p. 151: Jeff Gross/Getty Images; p. 152: Dominic Cooley

CHAPTER 10: THE BIG JUMP
pp. 157, 160-161, 163: Lars Gange/rally.subaru.com; pp. 158-159: Malcolm McCassy, pp. 159,
168-169: Pastrana family collection; p. 162: Stephane de Sakutin/AFP/Getty Images; p. 164:
Ron Meredith; p. 165: Richard Miaskiewicz/Atomic Motorsport Concepts; p. 173: Matt Ware

First of all, thanks to my sponsors, for their support and friendship over the years—Roger DeCoster, Pat Alexander, and Mel Harris at Suzuki Motorcycles, which has been with me since the beginning; Ken Block and DC Shoes; Jeff Fox and Victor Sheldon at Thor; Jeff Cernic, for supporting me no matter what I do; Andy Bell and Cam McQueen at Ogio; Dane Herron and the team at Red Bull; Gregg Godfrey, Jeremy Rawle, and the entire Nitro Circus crew; Gabriele Mazzarolo and Malcolm McCassy at Alpinestars; James Hahn at Subaru; Lance Smith, Christian Edstrom, and the guys at Vermont Sports Car; Mark Phares at Smith Optics; the folks at Nixon Watches, Kicker, and Studio 411; Todd Lentz at EVS Sports; Charlie Mancuso at Live Nation.

My agent Steve Astephen, Travis Clarke, and everyone else at Wasserman Media Group, for knowing where I am when I don't even know where I am.

A special thank you to ESPN, ESPN Books, and everyone from the X Games for providing me a platform to perform on.

My friends, for too many stories to fit into one book—Kenny Bartram, Jim DeChamp, Mad Mike Jones, Ronnie Renner, Todd Jacobs, Todd Lentz, Robby Reynard, Ron Meredith, Hubert "Fluffer" Rowland, Jolene, Nicole, and Billy … I wish I had space to name you all.

Above all, to my fans everywhere who have supported me from the beginning, thank you.

And to anyone I am forgetting, it's not that I don't love you. I've just hit my head too many times.

—T.P.

It's amazing what you can accomplish with the help of supportive friends and dedicated workaholics, fueled by a spark of inspiration—and a few beers after work on a Wednesday. But if it takes a village to raise a Motocross star, it takes a nation to write and publish a book. This particular story could not have been told without the help of many folks working behind the scenes. So let's bring them front and center.

The sparks, Shaun Assael and Peter Keating, for helping a colleague turn incomplete thoughts into a really good idea.

ESPN The Magazine senior deputy editor Steve Malley, for jumping on board and making every page better—and 20% shorter.

The ESPN Books department, for taking The Big Jump. Literally. ESPN Books and Magazine chief Gary Hoenig and managing editor Perry van der Meer, who green-lighted a project that would keep one Mag employee impossibly busy, yet made her term of dual employment impossibly easy. Editor Michael Solomon who, from the very beginning, encouraged me to make an indecent (book) proposal. To Chris Raymond, Sandy DeShong, Jessica Welke, John Glenn, and Ellie Seifert … thank you.

A very special thank you to Linda "I can, no, I will find that photo" Ng.

Researcher Melissa Malamut, for her constant reminders that phonetic spellings aren't necessarily correct spellings. And copy editor Beth Adelman, for that fine-tooth comb.

Designers Mike Joyce and Henry Lee, for breathing life into an overly ambitious idea.

Michelle Lindsay, for her marketing genius and friendship.

Steve Astephen, who always took the time to check that blinking red light on his BlackBerry and return frantic e-mails. And Travis Clarke for his GPS-like TP-tracking abilities.

Frank R. Scatoni and Greg Dinkin at Venture Literary, for guidance.

The holders of photos and information, for releasing them and asking for nothing more than a sincere thank you in return. Thank you. Sincerely. The book would be thinner without your memories—Mat Hoffman, Allen Kee, Ron Meredith, Malcolm McCassy, Nicole Mancuso, Ryan Sheckler, Ronnie Renner, Kenny Bartram, Bob Burnquist, Greg Powell, and the entire Pastrana family.

And, of course, Travis Pastrana, for your endless stories worthy of inspiring others—and for packing a damn good parachute. Can't make the sequel without you.

—A.R.

Travis Pastrana is the most celebrated freestyle motocross athlete in history. At 14, he became the youngest World Freestyle Motocross champion, and at 23, he became the youngest American rally car champion. Although his career takes him around the world, he is most happy at home in Davidsonville, Maryland, where he is never more than five minutes from his grandma's house.

Alyssa Roenigk is an editor and writer at *ESPN The Magazine.* Her work covering action sports has led her into countless acts of recklessness, including long-jumping a go-kart into Travis Pastrana's foam pit. A Floridian at heart and a Pennsylvanian by birth, she lives in New York City but spends little time at home.